THIRTY YEARS ON TRIAL

Kirk House Publishers
Burnsville, MN

THIRTY YEARS ON TRIAL
And Now a New Beginning

TAMICA BARNETT

First Printing: April 2026
First Edition

Paperback ISBN: 978-1-968428-25-9
eBook ISBN: 978-1-968428-27-3
Hardcover ISBN: 978-1-968428-26-6
LCCN: 2026910821

Interior and cover design by Ann Aubitz

Published by Kirk House Publishers
1250 E 115th Street
Burnsville, MN 55337
kirkhousepublishers.com
612-781-2815

TABLE OF CONTENTS

INTRODUCTION

On Monday, Tamica Barnett tried to tell Ramsey County Judge Peterson how it feels to have her mother killed by her stepfather. "I don't know why he did it," she sobbed as the judge looked on sympathetically. As 14-year-old Tamica returned to her seat in the courtroom, she walked past Preston Dillard, the 34-year-old man who killed her mother, who was also his wife. "I'll never forget you, Preston," she said.

Take my yoke upon you, and learn of me;
For I am meek and lowly in heart: and ye shall find rest unto your souls. – Mathew 11:29

CHAPTER 1
LIFE STARTED OUT VERY GOOD

Born in St. Paul, Minnesota, June 20, 1977, I was raised with two older brothers. Being the youngest of the bunch and the only girl "was very exciting," I must say. I remember that at three years of age, I attended Head Start. I graduated, proudly wearing my red-and-white cap and gown. Pictures from then show I was a good-looking kid.

When I was four, my father and mother decided they wanted to move out of Minnesota, so we moved to Peoria, Illinois, where my father's parents lived, as well as some of my mother's siblings. While on our way to our grandparents' house, we stopped at a place where our favorite chicken dish was on the menu. When we finally pulled up in front of their house, our grandmother was at the door greeting us with love.

"Our grandparents are the best," my brothers and I thought. Because we lived with our grandparents for a while, my mother and grandmother became best friends. My brothers and I loved living with our grandparents, because my grandmother was a baker. She used to bake peanut butter cookies, chocolate chip cookies, and butter cookies, which were my favorite. Cakes and pies were my brother's favorites. When my brothers knew that grandmother was about to bake a cake, they would wait to clean out the leftover cake mix from the bowl with their fingers—and eat it. Our grandfather was everything, he owned his own mechanic shop. My grandfather raised my father to work on cars, and my dad had a "golden wrench" because he was so good fixing cars. My mother loved the fact that my father had this skill. She never had to go anywhere other than to my father to get her car fixed.

Mother and grandmother had things in common, one was having the same religious beliefs. My grandmother was thrilled by the fact that my mother can sing—because she never heard her before, until one day when mother was singing in the bathroom. My grandmother heard her, and instantly she asked my mother to sing in the choir at her church. My mother, who does not have stage fright, replied yes.

That Sunday morning, we went to my grandmother's church. She introduced mother to the pastor, and told him that my mother can sing—and would like to lead the choir. Excited, the pastor agreed, so from that day on, Mother became the choir director. She had a beautiful set of vocal cords, and she continued singing and directing.

During the time we lived with our grandparents, my father taught me and my brother Carlos how to ride a bike. I fell a couple times, but that didn't stop me from learning. Because of my scratched-up knees, I should've called it quits, but I was determined to learn how to ride a bike. Carlos was a pro, and learned quickly. My big brother, Vell, was busy learning to drive, and Dad was teaching him.

CHAPTER 2
WHEN LIFE FELT RIGHT

At this point in our young lives, my brothers and I thought we had the most perfect life, living in a full-family household. My dad worked a part-time job, while also working beside my grandfather fixing cars. Mother had a job, cleaning hotel rooms, while at the same time also taking care of us. My brothers and I went to the best schools growing up.

Years down the line my father and mother moved us back to Minnesota. When my mother found out that my dad was cheating on her, she went to my grandmother and talked to her about it. My grandmother wasn't pleased to hear this about her son.

After we moved back to Minnesota, my dad still was cheating on my mother. She forgave him, and my father was good for a while. He decided that we'll start our lives all over again, in a different state. My mother agreed, so we moved to Kent, Washington.

CHAPTER 3
KENT, WASHINGTON, WAS A BIG CHANGE FOR US

My mother and father are now at ease, and my mother is happy again. Dad had already arranged housing for us before we moved there. Our living situation was never an issue for our parents. We moved into a three-bedroom apartment complex. I had my own room, but my brothers had to share a room. My father found a job right away, and started working for Red's Bike Shop. My brothers and I were excited about our father's new job because we got new bikes. I actually had two bikes, a 10-speed and a regular Rainbow Bright dirt bike. I was so spoiled; sometimes the youngest gets everything. My brothers, now 8 and 15, had all the action figures, like GI Joes, Spiderman and Superman. They even had train sets and Atari video games. Donkey Kong was one of my favorite games, so was Pac Man.

At age 8, I started making friends in the complex. My friends and I played all the time, and shared the same interests. We loved Barbies, and Cabbage Patch dolls. My dad bought me an Easy Baked Oven, a little girl's dream in the '80. We had it all—until my father's mistress found out where we lived. She kept causing drama by bothering my mother. My mother often had to deal with phone calls from my father's "side-chicks"—and the words that the side-chicks used to say weren't pleasant. At that point, my mother was fed up.

Unfortunately, our father had women he had been with in Illinois, and elsewhere, and our mother had been tolerant and put on a happy face. Now, however, our mother and father were splitting up, which was sad news to our ears. My mother was so stressed out, she called her sister who also lived in Washington. She asked her sister if she could watch over us while she goes back to Minnesota to clear her mind. She stayed in Minnesota for two weeks and made her decision.

Our mother decided to move us back to Minnesota, and she had found out that my dad had other children there—my brothers and I have never met them before. All we knew was that *our family was broken.*

My father was a "rolling stone"—and "home" was wherever he hung his hat. Although my father wasn't a loyal man to my mother, he was a good father to us. Mother rented a bedroom from her sister for two months, until she found housing for us. Mother soon did, and my brothers and I are happy because we were used to being in our own home.

Alarming Statistics from U.S. Census Bureau and other studies showed:

- Before 1970, Black women were more likely to be married than white women. (This was no longer true when I was young.)

- Share of births to unwed Black mothers in 2019 was 70 percent.
- Marriage reduces poverty for Black families from 7 percent to 35.6 percent.
- Boys (24-32) from intact families are 36 percent more likely never go to prison, and 19 percent likely to graduate college.
- Boys of single Black mothers, it's 15 percent.

CHAPTER 4
"PRINCE CHARMING" ENTERS OUR LIFE

Once we were settled in our new home, Mother is finally happily breathing again. We reunited with family and friends, having big gatherings as the vibes are good. Mother is now at the stage where she feels she is ready to date. Happy as ever, mother is smiling from ear to ear, which made us happy for her. Mother then finds her Prince Charming, who had a glass-slipper trail. We haven't seen our mom this happy in a long time, after the split-up between her and our father. My brothers and I haven't met him yet, because "I guess" mother wasn't ready for us to meet the man of her dreams.

Early one Saturday morning, my brothers and I are still asleep. Mother is up cleaning, listening to her gospel music, and singing like she always does. My brothers and I woke up smelling the strong scent of Pine-Sol® traveling through the house. We were getting ready for the day when mother called us into the kitchen and excitedly tells us that her friend is coming over today. As strange as it sounded to us, we went along with it. Shortly after, mother's friend arrives, he walks in and introduces himself, saying with a smile, "I'm Preston."

My brothers and I smiled back and introduced ourselves. As time went on, Preston seemed cool, buying us things. We had the latest fashion, the first kids to have a cell phone and other flashy items in elementary school, so we thought we were big shots.

Preston was a guy with money from Chicago, so we thought he was rich. Preston had three cars, and he taught my brother Carlos how to drive a stick shift. The car model was a 1989 Nova, burnt orange to be exact. Carlos thought he was doing big things, because he was driving at the age of 11—which really was pretty cool back in the 1980's.

Mother was pleased that Preston took care of us for the most part. She thought she'd *found the one,* and we thought she had, too. Preston started to bring in more items, from new clothes to new shoes. Now my brothers and I are starting to wonder: How can he afford all the nice things with no job? *We found out later he was a drug dealer.* Preston sold crack cocaine, and he also used it himself. During his use, things started to change for the worse as crack cocaine was starting to take over Preston's mind.

Now being around Preston was like walking on a tightrope—one wrong word or action could quickly tip things to turn into a major chaos.

Preston started to get abusive, swearing and yelling around the house. Two weeks into their relationship, he beat Carlos and me with a belt—all because we didn't do what he said right away. We lived in a duplex apartment. Carlos and I befriended the kids downstairs. My mother became friends with the woman of the house, only to find out that she was sister to Preston's other girlfriend.

One day I risked saying, "Mom, Preston hurts you and us kids too often—for no reason. That's not right. You have to leave him." But she didn't!

I know all this because as a child of age ten, I was observant. Our older brother moved out on his own because he didn't get along with Preston. Now my mom, Carlos and I, were alone with Preston. The verbal abuse had reached a point where Preston is now making threats—which quickly shifted into physical abuse. Mother is now scared. Preston had our mother so scared of him because he knew he had power and full control of her mind. In his own mind, Preston had so much control that he thought it was okay to bring his other girlfriend around—and for some odd reason, our mother was okay with it. Confused, she was living in fear, walking around with invisible bruises. Her body is covered with extra clothing, so she can hide the marks Preston had put on her. Carlos and I are aware of the marks on her body, because we witnessed and experienced first-hand the abusive things he did to us. I'm pretty sure Preston was abusing her while we were at school. He could do a lot of things—but he couldn't stop his abusive ways.

And God saw that the wickedness of men was great in the earth
And that every imagination of the thoughts was evil continually.
– Genesis 6:5

On the last day of school, brother Carlos, exactly a year older than me, and I came home from school to greet our mother. Happily going up the stairs, we opened the front door to greet her. Carlos and I looked into our mother's eyes, and seeing a scared look on her face, we knew something was wrong. The front door remained open, and as we looked back to close it, Preston comes from behind the door with a belt, and instantly starts to beat us. Carlos and I are confused, wondering how can this be, as the belt lashes across our poor little bodies while we're hollering for mercy—not knowing what we did wrong. Mother sat on the couch with big alligator tears running down her cheeks, explaining through her eyes how sorry she is for what has happened to us. Thinking ahead, I said to myself, "It's about to be a roller coaster…."

At ages 10 and 11, Carlos and I witnessed our mother get beat up on several occasions. Our big brother Vell, who is five and six years older than us, was at home with his own family. He had heard the news about Preston abusing us and came right over, filled with anger, and ready to fight Preston about the awful things that he was hearing. Preston and my big brother Vell got into a physical fight, where blood was shed and bones broken.

Mother started to wear sunglasses to hide the black eyes from family and friends, but they knew what was going on because of her and us kids' changed behavior.

Mother stopped talking on the phone, and she stopped coming to family gatherings—all signs of abuse in the household.

I wondered then, and still wonder now, why did this man's words always carry more weight   with my mother—than her own words. I also worried how I was going to prevent turning to and being dependent on such a horrible man in my own relationships. I am starting to fear I would be sad and lonely, and follow in Mom's path—and would put up with any man I met, even if he abused me emotionally or physically.

One day when I came home from school, I thought I had seen a statue standing in front of our house. With my vision being a little blurry because of the bright shining sun, I couldn't clearly see what it was. As I got closer, it was not a statue—it was my brother Carlos standing outside in front of a tree wearing winter gear, such as snow hat, boots, snow pants, and a coat in 85-degree weather. This was a punishment that Preston decided he should have. I walked up to Carlos and gave him a hug; then we cried together. I called my dad that very next day to inform him of what went on. He drove from Peoria, Illinois, to where we lived in Minnesota, to ask some questions. Of course, Preston denied everything—and our mother sat silently, too scared to say if it's true or not. *She didn't open her mouth one time to protect us.*

From then on, I knew we were in serious danger.

All those gathered here will know that it is not by sword

Or spear that the Lord saves; for the battle is the Lord's.

– David 17:47

Now we are asking each other when this is going to stop. I plotted to take matters into my own hands. I found out Carlos had a .38 caliber handgun in the house. He had already turned "to the streets" at age 13, and had become part of a local gang. That's where he got the gun! When I asked him to let me see the gun, he asked why. I replied, "Mom is at work, Preston is in the room sleeping. I'm about to kill him." Of course, he agreed to let me use it, so he gave it to me. I walked upstairs, went through the kitchen to their bedroom where the door was cracked halfway open. I quietly opened the door a little more to get the perfect aim. Carlos stood behind me as I cocked the gun while

Preston was sound asleep in the bed. I put my hands on the trigger, ready to fire, thinking I can end this abuse. Before I can fire, Carlos whispers "Tamica, please don't do it."

It had taken everything in me not to end Preston's life, especially when I had the opportunity to kill him. All I was thinking and saying at that time was, "Carlos, I'm eleven and you're twelve. If I kill him now, we'll get out of jail when we turn 18 years old.

The other shocking thing was that during this time, Preston and Mother were quietly and secretly married—we didn't know anything about it—and *now he was her husband!!!* It is disturbing being a child living in an abusive home, plotting murder against their mother's husband who is not the father of either child.

Of course, the abuse didn't stop. Mother was at a point in her life now that she is frightened by her husband's strange behavior. When Preston discovered that he had put fear in our mother, the abuse occurred on a regular basis, like it was his hobby.

The abuse is now out of control and very beyond our understanding. Carlos and I also started getting beat with wrestler's weight belts, stun guns, and regular leather belts.

Summer was over, and now school is in session. As children, age 12 and 13, Carlos and I have now *taken our trauma to school with us.* We started to get in trouble at school for not following directions, getting sent to detention, and having to stay after school sometimes. On this particular day, I was suspended from school for punching the principal; I was in the fourth grade at the time. The school I attended made that phone call home to my mother, and she was asked to come pick me up because I have been suspended for assault.

Preston and my mother came to pick me up. At home, Preston told my mom to beat me for getting in trouble in school. My mother looked me in the eyes with such pain, hurt and fear.

I could tell she didn't want to beat me, but he yelled and threatened her saying, "If you don't beat her, I'm going to beat you."

I looked at my mother, laid down across the bed and said to her, "Momma, go on and beat me so he won't beat you,"—and she did just that with tears running down her face.

I couldn't understand why she was putting up with these *three years of non-stop abuse*. Things were getting more dangerous every day.

Preston made my mother, Carlos and me sit in the kitchen in a circle. He put a skillet on top of the stove and filled it with cooking oil, turning the burner on as high as it can go. He walks around us in this circle with an evil look on his face, and his eyes were filled with darkness.

When Mother started to cry, he stopped to look at her and said, "If you don't tell your kids the truth, I'll throw this hot oil in your face. Her voice cracks from crying, trying to get the words out—but silence is all we heard. I jumped out of my chair with force and might like I've never had before. At 12 years of age, I spoke these words to Preston, saying, "If you throw that hot grease in my mother's face, I'll kill you!"

I ran out of the house knocked on the nearest neighbor's door, asking if they could call the police. When the police came, Preston was arrested for assault on my mother.

Preston was in jail for quite some time. Life was good, too. Mother was happy, and she came around the family more, opening up and venting to her sister. The more she opened up, the more her life became peaceful.

As time went on, Mother became strong…which lasted for as long as it could.

CHAPTER 5
EVERYTHING CHANGES...

Suddenly the phone rings, and when mother picks it up, the operator on the other end says, "You have a collect call from Preston." We paused, seeing that the look on her face *was all about loneliness and loyalty.*

She accepted the phone call, and they talked almost every day after that. Preston knew if he could get her to talk to him, he'd win her back, which of course HE DID!

Carlos and I are talking to each other, trying to figure it out. *How can a woman talk to a man who causes harm to us like it's a normal way of life?*

A few months later, just when we thought Preston was out of our lives, we heard a knock on the door that sounded strange and hollow. When Mother opens the door, our mouths drop to the floor in disbelief—it's the beast, Preston. Carlos and I were in shock, shaking our heads.

Preston charmed his way back into my mother's arms, and she fell for it. Now we're back to square one: the abuse, torture, black eyes, threats to our mother, plus Carlos and I were also abused. The list goes on.

Even as a child, I learned these important things from what I had witnessed: 1) If your conscience speaks, don't silence it—listen. 2) Always listen to that little voice that tells you something isn't right, and 3) Love can't live where there's humiliation.

With Preston being the beast that he is, he had found a way to have our mother alone. He had made false accusations to the juvenile court division, lying, saying things about the need for my brother and me to be sent away. Very sadly it worked because of our behavior in school. We only acted out because of what was going on in our household, but people in the courts really didn't know. Carlos and I felt like they seemed not to care anyhow, so we really never talked about it.

Looking back, we realized that the "system" to protect children listened to a man who had "an order of protection" against him to stay away from our mother—and us. They didn't check out anything and they simply listened to HIM!!

CHAPTER 6
TAKEN FROM OUR MOTHER AT AGES 13 AND 14

I'm sent to St. Croix Camp, a juvenile facility in Hinckley, Minnesota, and I served three months there. St. Croix Camp is where juveniles are sent for their bad behavior. However, I couldn't be released without completing my treatment plan. It sucked because for our punishment, we had to chop wood. The camp wasn't a locked-up facility, so you were free to run away. During my stay at the camp, I had peers who were planning to run away from the camp—and it sounded good to me, so I joined them. We waited until night to plan the escape when the staff was busy doing other things, like changing shift. We slipped by them and ran towards the woods, but I paused and the girls went on ahead of me. All I could think about was mountain lions and bears getting me in the woods.

I headed back to the camp, knowing I was about to get punished. I didn't care because chopping wood is better than being attacked by a bear. I had to chop 30 tree logs into six-inch lengths for firewood. It taught me a lesson: never try to escape.

The others were found sometime later and received a harsher punishment. It's unlikely they won't be doing that again.

Although this punishment sucked, I've learned about following rules—and staying out of trouble. However, this camp for kids with discipline problems also included events they called "expos," and with a group of my peers, we all piled on a bus and traveled to see the Black Hills and Mt. Rushmore in South Dakota, and another trip to Canada where I learned to downhill ski and ice skate. We were also camping in Superior National Forest, a part of the Boundary Waters Region along the border of Minnesota and Ontario, Canada. In between this all, I learned how to shear sheep—a good skill if you're a farmer.

We also had to do a "solo," where you spent three nights and four days camping alone in the dense woods. This challenge had to be passed before you were considered "ready to go home." So in addition to seeing new places, and having new experiences, I learned survival tips, discipline, rules—and I gained a lot of self-confidence.

Carlos was sent to Boys Totem Town in St. Paul, Minnesota where he served over six months. The boys' home where Carlos was sent was similar to the camp I was in. The only thing different was that he didn't chop wood for punishment. Punishment there was having time added to their stay.

During the time we were absent from home, Mother was by herself, but not totally. I'm pretty sure she had family around her sometimes.

As our absence is obvious, mother is being abused more and more. Now the police are called the majority of the time for domestic assault on her. Carlos and I weren't present but we heard afterwards about what our mother was going through while we were away.

Mother went to visit her father who lived a couple miles away—to get some fresh air—but somehow Preston found out where she was. She didn't want to talk to him when he called my grandfather's house to speak with her. Now Preston gets upset and as his anger flairs up, and he goes to my grandfather's house where he kicks in the front door—and proceeded to get at our mother.

When the police were called, Preston ran away before they arrived. My mother and grandfather filed a report, and now Preston had a warrant out for him as he was charged with breaking and entering; then attempting to assault Mother.

The judge insisted that my mother get a restraining order against Preston who is a violent man, and then the judge signs off on the restraining order.

Carlos and I have been out of the home for quite some time now. During this time, Preston has put guns to her head, threatening to kill her if she tries to leave him. He also is stalking her, peeping through her windows at night. Every time mother sees him, she runs for her safety, but when she's in his presence, she starts shaking in fear and does what she is told.

My mother had been to court several times against Preston about his violating the restraining order. Preston seemed not to care...*it's like he wanted it his way*.

CHAPTER 7
CARLOS AND I RETURN HOME

Carlos and I are both back at home now, having served our time in juvenile lockup. We were so happy to see our mom because she never came to visit us. We weren't worried about a visit; we were just happy to see our mom.

Preston is still around causing damage to our home, and continues being the beast that he is, walking around with smoke coming from his nose, and a wicked smirk on his face. We are wondering: *Why won't our mom leave this man?*

The beatings of Carlos and me continued, making us troubled teens trying to find our place in life—trying to understand this life, and causing us not to come home as we were told.

Why, oh why, did that man's voice always carry more weight with her than her own words.

CHAPTER 8
PRESTON GETS US SENT AWAY AGAIN—AND THEN EXPLODES

t ages 14 and 15, Preston finds another way to get us sent away again. He called the courts, told them we've been acting up at home, not listening and being disobedient towards our mother— which had some truth, but not all. Soon the probation officers removed us from our home again.

Again, Carlos and I had this big question: How can the legal system, especially the juvenile officials, believe a man who already had been in jail for domestic violence, and also had a restraining order against him—and they do not check the truth and reality that exists in this household? Thinking about that made us feel like "helpless children" no one cares about.

This time I was sent up to Woodland Hills, another place where we cut wood. October 31, 1991, is the first day I entered Woodland Hills to start my treatment plan. My mother and a Probation Officer dropped me off. Hugging my mother goodbye, I was crying my eyes out because she had to leave me there. During my stay at Woodland Hills, Carlos is in St. Croix Camp, where I had been earlier, before I was moved to Hinckley, Minnesota.

All hell breaks loose, and Preston is now on a rampage, plotting his next move. My mother is at home alone very scared, but she finally gets brave enough to make a sad-but-true police report of all the harm Preston had done to her. "He's going to kill me," she reported. Shortly after that, she had contacted some of the family in Peoria, Illinois, saying that she's moving back to start all over again.

Mother started to pack her things, getting ready for this big move. She notified our probation officer to inform her that she's moving out of state—and would like to take us with her. My mother called the staff at Woodland Hills, and told them of her plan.

The staff walked into my dorm room to tell me the news— exciting news that my ears were pleased to hear. Mother decided to have some of the family members move in with her, while Carlos and I were away because she needed to feel safe. Mother had two of my older cousins and their nine-year-old daughter move in.

Preston came over and asked my mother for money so he could buy crack cocaine. Mother stressed to him she doesn't have it. Preston approached her again around 12:30 a.m. March 1, 1992, once more demanding money.

As Preston gets extremely angry and violent when she said, "Preston, I don't have any money," and quickly he reached into his pocket. Mother is sitting on the side of her bed when he pulled out a pocket knife and stabbed her under her breast.

Mother jumped up from her position in the bed, screamed and said, "Why Preston?" When she walks out of her room, Preston runs around her, and rushes out the front door. Mother is holding her heart and walks down the stairs. She reached for the phone and called 911, to report that Preston had stabbed her. Mother also reported saying to the police, "I'm not going to make it this time!"

Mother collapsed onto the floor, her family surrounded her until the ambulance arrived to take her to the hospital, where she died later.

Unfortunately, my nine-year-old cousin had witnessed Mother's murder as she was the only one awake at that time.

A dark gloom spread over the neighborhood when it was whispered from one to another that the young wife and mother was gone, died by the violent hand of her new husband.

CHAPTER 9
THE DAY OUR LIVES CHANGED FOREVER

Sunday March 1, 1992, at 3:00 a.m., was the day our lives changed. Preston was arrested for the murder of his wife, our mother.

At the camps, it's Sunday around 5:00 p.m. when we can call our parents, or the parents call their kids. It's getting late, and I'm starting to wonder why mother hasn't called me. I'm noticing all the others are getting phone calls from their parents. When I ask the staff if my mother has called yet, they replied no, but with a worrisome look in their eyes.

When I walked out of the office, the staff followed behind me into my room. They looked at me with tears in their eyes and said, *"Tamica, I'm so sorry to tell you that Preston murdered your mother."* I looked at the staff in disbelief and asked with a chuckle, "Are you sure"? They replied, "Yes, Tamica your cousin called to tell us."

In shock, my body felt like a balloon had popped inside me, confused about what my ears just heard. I'm weak at the knees, feeling them collapse as I stand stiff with pain.

The staff surrounded me, crying for me while trying to get me to calm down. My breath is taken by hyperventilating, trying to make my brain register on what I just heard.

Shortly after the staff told me about my mother being murdered, the staff drove me to Hinckley, Minnesota, to meet up with my brother. Carlos and I hadn't seen each other in five months—until this sad day. As I stepped out of the van, Carlos was already standing outside of his van. We ran up to one another and held each other tight, crying our eyes out. I whispered to Carlos in pain, saying, "See, if you wouldn't have stopped me from killing Preston, Mom would still be here."

Our family came to pick us up so we could be with them in this time of mourning. Carlos and I met up with our older brother, Vell, who was also extremely emotionally torn apart because he had been at the hospital with Mom took her last breath. In fact, I heard he tried to lift her up off the exam table at the hospital, yelling, "Momma, no, don't leave us!" Sad as it was, we are now planning a funeral for our mother.

Days later, a day we'll remember forever…Carlos and I now stood alone by Mother's casket, holding hands so tightly as if we'll never let go. Carlos said, "Mom, why did you stay with that horrible man. It seemed you no longer loved him—but were in total fear for yourself—and Tamica and me."

Then I said, "Why Mom, why?" We love you so, and now you are no longer here for us to love, to teach us, to protect us, and to depend on. How are we going to survive without you in this world?"

Friends, family, and others walked up to Carlos and me, almost wordless, and most could only say, "I'm sorry, kids." Some added things like: "I had no idea this was happening to your mother—and to both you kids."

Now that the funeral is over with, I had to go back to Woodland Hills as I had three more months left to finish. During those three months, they recommended I start attending grieving classes as Preston's court date was being prepared. I had to go to the funeral home, which I didn't like because it's scary. They wanted me to learn about death, but I didn't want to learn. It was too much for me at that time.

Now it has been two weeks since my mother's death, and the staff members are preparing me for court the next day. We leave Duluth, Minnesota, and drive down to St. Paul where the hearing took place. This is the first time in six months that I have seen Preston. With court now in session, the prosecutor started calling witnesses to the stand—and she called my name first. As I approached the bench, Judge Peterson thought it wasn't a good idea for me to testify. He also suggested that my nine-year-old cousin, who was the witness, *not* take the stand either. They took matters in their own hands, figuring they had enough evidence to charge Preston with second degree murder.

Judge Peterson looks down at Preston. He asked him if there was anything that he would like to say before he made his ruling. Preston replied yes. He said to the court, "The death of my wife caused me much pain."

Judge Peterson looked at Preston and said, "You should understand my sympathy today is not with you." Then he said to Preston with a soft but harsh voice, "My sympathy is with her children and family."

I was wise in my youth; I had written a victim impact statement. I was asked to read it before the courts and to Preston.

I said to Preston, "It hurts with no mom. Look, you took an angel out…my mom was the beauty and you were the beast." As tears rolled down my face, I told Preston that now he has to deal with God.

Preston spoke in a soft monotone, and showed no emotion as he entered the plea of unintentional second-degree murder. In 1992, Preston was sentenced to 25 years in prison, with state guidelines to serve over half of his time. (He was released in 2009, having met that guideline.)

Years later, I learned that:
- Every year an estimated **15 million children are exposed to domestic violence.**
  - Source National Task Force to End Sexual and Domestic Abuse
- **3.3 million children** in the U.S. *witness violence* against a female in their family — their mother or female caretaker.
- Domestic violence is a global problem. An estimated **51,100 women and girls were killed by their intimate partners or family members in 2023.** This translates to an average of 140 women and girls murdered each day by someone they know, often a man.

- o These figures, collected by UN Women_and the UN Office on Drugs and Crime, likely represent an undercount due to inconsistent reporting worldwide.
- **The age statistics are shocking**:
  - o In 2023, around 2,444 homicide victims in the United States were aged between 20 and 24 years old.
  - o An additional 2,362 murder victims were between the ages of 30 and 34 years old.
  - o Most murder victims in the United States in 2023 were between the ages of 17 and 54 years old.
- Source, Statista Research Department, Nov. 7, 2024

CHAPTER 10
OUR LIVES CHANGED...
AND NOT FOR THE BETTER

After I completed my stay at Woodland Hills, I was sent to live with my aunt. While getting adjusted to the way she lived, my brother Carlos and I were separated. He lived with my other aunt, but we saw each other every day. Carlos and I stood by one another through thick and thin, never missing a beat.

My extended family was dysfunctional—there was no discipline in the homes.

During my stay at my aunt's house, at age 15, I was manipulated by a man I had no business being with. *I was looking for love in the wrong places* after I lost my mom to murder. This man was much older than me, but my aunt didn't seem to care. I thought that it was okay to lay up with this man, because nobody said it was wrong. I was a minor, became pregnant and had a miscarriage. Once the situation was over, I realized it was wrong. My mother didn't raise me to be this way. He was the father of one of my cousin's kids, and if I knew what I know today, it would have never happened.

With us having no guidance, we chose "the streets"—to feel important—and feel like we belonged somewhere. When I was 16 and Carlos was 17, we joined two different gangs, and I fell in with a group of kids who made me feel like I belonged somewhere. We started to change *big time*, and we began selling drugs. Being out all night in the streets is all we knew. We felt as though no one cared about us, not even our big brother. Carlos and I had love for the streets, where we were getting paid to sell drugs. It was the thing to do back then to make fast money.

Now I'm 17 years old, and I started dating and soon became pregnant. When I had my son on April 4, 1995, I named him Kavion and was one happy mother. But it wasn't long before Kavion's father disappeared back to the streets as a drug dealer and a gang member. However, *I still wanted to be on the streets*, even after I had my first baby. My aunt was taking care of the baby, and I felt like I was free—free to do whatever I wanted to do. I took complete advantage of it, too, having often been "on the streets" occasionally since age 12-13. Truth is that since Preston had come into our lives and our home, *we did NOT want to be there*.

I had started skipping school, often ran away from home to the "streets," and was always in trouble at school. This is what caused me to be sent by school authorities to these juvenile detention places. The streets were my second home until I was about 20.

My aunts tried to do their best for us. The only mistake was *there was no discipline*. We weren't used to this kind of parenting, as we were raised from a different cloth. One thing for certain, my aunt made sure we've always had a place to stay, and always had food in the fridge and in the deep freezer. My aunt asked to have temporary custody of my infant son…*because at age 18, I still wanted to party*—it was a choice I made, but not because I was a bad mother.

My son's dad already had multiple women and kids, so it wasn't serious between us—he was just my sperm donor. As a young girl, I was manipulated by being with a popular drug dealer, and I didn't care, because he had lots of money and nice cars.

Looking back, what did I gain by being on the street, and all that partying? In my mind, we were safer on the streets than in our own home with Preston living there. Or…*Was I looking for love in all the wrong places?*

CHAPTER 11
THINGS CHANGED
WHEN I WAS 19

As I faded away from being on the streets, I was 19. I started to chill out, trying to understand my place in life—*and beginning to understand how serious motherhood is.* I finally got things halfway in order. I moved out of my aunt's place and moved into my own apartment, where I started dating a guy.

Out of lust, I thought he was the one for me, only to find out he was a cheater. However, one good thing came out of this relationship. I became pregnant with my first daughter who was born premature. Her father was so proud—because she was his first kid. His family loved her, and I never had her at home with me as she mostly stayed over at their house. The guy and I stopped seeing each other because it wasn't working out, so I moved on.

A year went by, and I am now 20 years old, with two children, ages two and three. Single, not wanting to date for a while until one day I'm at home watching movies when I get a knock on the door. It was my cousin asking if she and a few of her friends can come in. I instantly said no, but then I changed my mind. My cousin has this guy with her. He was very attractive, so I approached him, and from there, our relationship took off.

One day my brother Carlos comes to my house, and he sees my friend Ricky. Surprisingly, they knew each other from being in juvenile detention. It was a party from there.

We started dating for a while, and I became pregnant sometime later. We've been blessed with a baby girl, and we became a couple. "Bonnie and Clyde" was the name for us, because we were always doing everything together.

Things started to get very serious between us, so Ricky finally took me to meet his mother. I thought his mother was mean at first, as her speech was bold—only to find out she was sweet. A year has passed, and now I gave birth to my second daughter, our second child together. From that day on, our bond is like glue. We moved into our first apartment together.

My brother Carlos always came over, and happily he also had his own family. He was in love with his high school sweetheart. She became pregnant and gave birth to a beautiful baby girl. Carlos was so excited it was his first baby, "spoiled" wasn't the word, but she had everything. Now that Carlos and I are happier in our lives, things are a little easier for us. We still held onto one another, and we never forgot what we've been through together. We were like two peas in a pod.

CHAPTER 12
CARLOS GETS INTO TROUBLE

A few years went by, and Carlos and his high school sweetheart had called it quits. Carlos moved in with me, and stayed for a year off and on, until he found his own home. Moving into his own home didn't work out so well, so he moved back in with us. *He had my back, and I had his.*

The next morning Carlos woke up, took a shower and dressed for the day. He came in where I was and said he'd be back later. I said, "Okay," but I didn't see him until the next day at 7:00 p.m., because he had snuck down to Peoria, Illinois, to get our father. I was surprised to see our father. We saw our father off and on for years. We didn't mind because our father had a sick wife he had to take care of. Our father stayed with us for a while, as Thanksgiving was approaching. We had a good Thanksgiving dinner, until my brothers got into an altercation. The police were called because it became out-of-hand. After that incident, Carlos left the house to call me. He's crying on the other line as I cried with him. He says to me, "Tamica, I'm tired of people taking things from me," I say back to him, "Let's pray about it, Brother." He replies, "That has nothing to do with it."

A few days later it's getting late, and when the sun goes down, Carlos came over with a few of his friends around 9:00 p.m. We sat around the table, had a few beers and chatted. Carlos is acting mighty strange, but I thought nothing of it. We continued to chat for a while. Now it's 10:30 p.m., and Carlos and his friends are ready to leave. They stood up from the table and proceeded out the door. Carlos came right back upstairs, and he opened the front door, standing in between my apartment and the hallway. I asked him, "Did you forget something, Brother?" He replies, "No Sister, I didn't," as he leaves out the door.

The next morning, I woke up happy. The date is November 29, 2001, and I'm getting ready to put up the Christmas tree. My phone rings, and I answer with joy. On the other end of the phone line all I could hear was crying and yelling. It was a friend of the family. I asked her, "What's wrong? Did something happen?" When she replied saying, "I'm sorry." I asked, "Sorry for what?" She replies, saying with pure sadness, "Carlos is dead, I'm in shock."

I'm thinking I was just with him last night. My father is in the other room hearing me scream, wondering what's going on. When I told him Carlos is dead, my dad was shocked with disbelief. He asks, "What happened?" I didn't know at that time—but all I knew was Carlos, my best friend, was gone. We found out minutes later what was the cause of his death, sadly he was shot in the head three times. When I asked the friend of the family where he was located, she told me. My big brother, father and I went to the murder scene. We see a crowd of many people standing around sobbing. I look over to the side and see

Carlos' car with a hearse pulled next to it. I was in so much pain. The coroners were holding sheets up, blocking the view of his body while they pulled him out of his car. I couldn't believe what I was witnessing, confused about why someone would want to kill him. As the coroner takes his body away, reality sets in.

With my mother already gone, I didn't know what to do, but I knew I had to step up to plan a funeral for my brother. My father, confused and in shock, said to me, "Tamica, my son came to get me for his funeral." My dad started to cry—I had never seen my dad cry before. It was unusual, but I knew my father was really hurting. We are all deeply mourning the loss of Carlos. After a couple of hours pass, the phone rings. It's the medical examiner asking me to come view Carlos' body. My dad, brother and I, with some family members, went to the mortuary. We walked in, and the examiners took me into the room where the body was. I saw my brother on the table with his eyes halfway open. He had a shocking look on his face, like he knew his killer.

I had to bury my 24-year-old brother. It was hard, but I did what he would do for me. Now that the date is set to bury Carlos, my last stop was to get his outfit for the day of viewing. One of my cousins met me there so she could braid his hair. I watched as she began to part his hair. She did one cornrow; then broke out with tears. She continued, but I understood the pain.

The mother of Carlos' only child became sick with sadness and grief after his death. They were planning to get back together, and I felt sorry for her. As I grabbed to hug her, she collapsed in my arms. She's screaming in pain the words, "Why, why, why?" as I held her so she didn't fall.

The next day I had to visit the funeral home to pick out Carlos's casket. From that day, I came to realize how strong God created me to be. One of my closest cousins joined me, because it was creepy for me to go by myself. Never in my life would I have imagined being the one to plan a funeral. At that time my mind was all over the place, with me thinking how am I going to pay for his funeral. The friend of the family suggested calling Help for Victims of Crime, an organization that helps pay for funeral costs up to $6,000 for victims of crime. I contacted them—and his funeral was paid for. They wrote a check that I gave to the funeral director the same day.

Now that the day of his funeral has arrived, I have butterflies that are out of this world. I prayed to God for strength, because reality has now taken its effect on me.

When I get to the funeral home, it's crowded with family and friends. They greet me with hugs and tears. I saw my father and my grandmother standing side by side. I go over and hug them, and my grandmother cries and says, "Oh Carlos' poor baby." My dad is trying his best to be strong for me, because he knew how much Carlos and I meant to each other—our birthdays are on the same day, June 20th—Carlos was born in 1976 and I was born on that day in 1977.

As I walked further into the funeral home, I noticed my big brother, who is crying his eyes out. Although Carlos and our big brother had a falling out before he died, I knew he still loved his little brother. However, my brothers never made peace before his death.

Now I'm viewing Carlos, as he's positioned stiff on his back. I walked up closer to the casket, touching his hands that felt like ice. I looked at him in disbelief, saying to myself…this is really my brother laying here cold. As I walk towards the back of the room I see my niece, Carlos' daughter. She was only six years old—so it wasn't clear to her what was really going on.

All she knew was that her father was asleep at that time. My family and friends expected me to spaz out, because of the tragedy. Where I come from, my God in heaven guided me. He gave me strength to do what my mother couldn't do. I couldn't have done this without my family support, I was only 24 years old. Now the service is almost over, the preacher is ending his message, and we were getting ready to go to the burial grounds.

I wanted Carlos to be buried close to our mother, however I didn't have enough money. It costs extra, so I stood up before we all went to the grave site and asked for donations to bury Carlos close to our mother. They supported my request, and enough money was donated to do what I asked, plus more. As the building is getting empty, the hearse pulls in front of the chapel. The pallbearers, three on each side, carry my brother's lifeless body and put him in the hearse. In front of me were two limos. I jumped in with my niece and her mother. I had money left over from the donation, so I kindly handed it over to her as my brother had only this one child. I didn't care or know how much it was— I just gave it to her.

Now we're on our way to the burial site, with a long line of cars trailing behind us. When we reached there, I knew this was the last time I was going to see my best friend.

RIP
Carlos L. Barnett
June, 20, 1976 – Nov, 29, 2001

Three weeks have gone by, and my feelings are still fresh about my brother's death. When I heard a knock on my door, I went to open it. An insurance man came in and explained that Carlos had taken out an insurance policy on himself. It was some good-looking numbers, and he left me as the beneficiary. As I thought about it, I remembered that we took out an insurance policy on each other, five months before his death. We agreed if something was to happen to either one of us, we'd take care of each other's kids. I kept my word, three months later an insurance check arrived in my mailbox. The most beautiful part about the arrival was, the check came on his daughter's seventh birthday—February 11, 2002. I can remember like it was yesterday. I contacted his daughter's mother and told her the good news. I met her and gave her part of the money. She ended up buying a house, I was so proud because through Carlos, I made it happen. He would have done the same for me, which my heart truly knew.

CHAPTER 13
RICKY AND I FINALLY WERE MARRIED

Things have become easier to deal with since Carlos' death. The heaviness eased and lifted up off my shoulders, trying to move on from things I can't change. However, after six months went by, I found myself getting involved in drugs, hanging around people I never met before—and we started having house parties, clubbing every night, and snorting cocaine. My kids' father had his own set of friends, but I had no idea he was using cocaine, too. When I found out that Ricky was using, I didn't care because I was using, too. So he and I came together, and he invited his friends and I invited my friends. We started having coke parties every night. We never had our kids around during these times of our unawareness. This went on for like a month straight. My kids' father and I are not paying attention to our relationship, and it was going down the drain due to our drug behavior. One morning Ricky woke me up, saying we need to stop—that the drugs and parties every night are destroying our family. I looked at him and said, "You're right. This is the end of our drug use."

After we stopped that day, we became closer than before, and we tied the knot. We didn't have a big wedding, and were married by a justice of peace. My father was present, and he gave me away. My cousin came and gave Ricky away. Shortly after we were married, our house caught on fire. Thanks be to God we weren't there; we were actually at his mother's house that night.

Some of our belongings were damaged, and the things that we could save, smelled like smoke.

It took us a couple days to clear out the house, but it was well worth it. We needed a fresh start anyways. After the fire, Ricky and I decided to move closer to his mother who lived in North Minneapolis, Minnesota. She had six other kids. I didn't know he had so many siblings, however; I thought it was cool. We rented out a room in his mother's house, and she treated me like family.

My oldest daughter was staying with her biological father, until I found housing. My oldest and only son stayed with my aunt for a while. Everything seemed to be getting back on track. I also found housing in North Minneapolis. My kids started school, and I never left the northside thereafter. When we were settled, my husband found a full-time job. I was a housewife, but I didn't mind because I had a working husband. He loved his little family, and we loved him too. Life was treating us good, and finally we were back on track. Soon after we found housing, and we moved into our own home. Living with his mother and siblings was interesting, and I had time to get to know them very well.

Soon after we were settled into our new home, we started having dinner parties. Ricky's family joined us, we came together as a whole, and "I was living the dream." I never thought, in a million years, that I could find someone to love me, and for me to equally love him back as a partner. We were inseparable, and I was loving my life.

My kids are going to school and everything is in order. I'm at home preparing dinner, because that's what a housewife does for her family. We started to prosper, buying new cars and having new furniture as we bounced back from the fire. My kids are well-maintained, clean and going to school every day. I was on Section 8, a low-income housing program. It made our lives a lot easier, and having food stamps also helped my family.

A few months went by, I saw some changes in my husband, changes that weren't good. We lived in a neighborhood that was drug-infested. My husband became part of the "hood" and started to sell marijuana. At first, I thought it was not okay, but then I figured…if I can't beat him; then I'll join him. My husband and I sold weed and became friends with some of the weed buyers. They would come over every day, to a point where they started having football tournaments on the Playstation2 video game. I even started playing, and I've become so good at playing Madden that people started to bet on me. We were still in our 20s, so it goes to show *my husband and I still had a little nonsense in us*.

This went on for months, until the police shut down the whole block where drugs were being sold. That still didn't change the fact that drugs are being sold. The north side of Minneapolis is compared to a certain area of Chicago, Illinois—including non-stop violence every day on the news. We stayed right on the block where it all took place, the drugs, crime, and murders. My husband knew about Minneapolis. Ricky grew up over there, I grew up in St. Paul across the Mississippi River, so I was brand new to the area.

We finally moved from there, moved in with his mother for the second time. The more I was around my husband's family, the more they became a part of me. I said to myself, "I love this family." I felt like I was a part of something. Getting introduced to every family member, I enjoyed watching his siblings grow up to have their own kids. I became Aunt Tammy to them, and my nieces and nephews treated me with love—like they were my own.

My husband and I finally moved out of his mother's house for the second time, and moved into our own space, but we were still a little immature. One day I decided that enough is enough. I spoke with my husband, saying it's time for us to grow up. We have kids that are growing up, and we need to be better role models for them. I understood that I have three daughters looking up to me, and a son who is looking up to my husband, his stepfather, as a "father figure." As time went on, we finally had our life in order, and we became better parents to our kids. My husband's uncle always came over to our house. He gave my kids treats, and money all the time. They loved their uncle, and I appreciated him because he took care of my older kids who weren't his nephews' children. I knew I was with the perfect man.

For those who desire to be rich, fall into temptations, and snares, and into many foolish and hurtful lusts, which drown men in degeneration and destruction.

-1st Timothy 6:9

My husband and I have been together for seven years. Now that I am deeper into his family, the real story is starting to unfold. The more I am around them, I'm seeing how divided his family is. Material things are all they cared about, and would cut any throat to stay on top. Material things and money became their God. They had become so caught up in appearance so that they forgot where they came from. My children started getting excluded. His mother had other grandchildren, and mine were the only grandchildren she left out. It was so bad that at a point, the other grandchildren thought they were better than my children. I knew all of this was happening because I wasn't a follower—I didn't want to do the things they were doing—so I became the opposite, and things started going down the drain from there; along with my marriage.

We still had our own home at that time, so I mostly stayed there. I understood that I was being tolerated by his family. On numerous occasions I was telling Ricky that his family doesn't like me. He always made excuses for them, especially his mother. I went along with it because talking to him about his family was like talking to a baby. I started to distance myself from being around his family. My husband still was working, and our kids are in school. I decided with time on my hands, I'm going back to school to get my GED—as I did not graduate high school.

I enrolled in school the very next day. It was so hard, but I wanted change. I wanted more in life, and I knew what my mother and father taught me as a child. When I started going to school, I was happy because the renewal of my mind was expanding. A couple of days went by, and one of my husband's family members approached me and said, "People are saying you're not going to finish school." I didn't take that remark lightly, but at the same time, I replied, "Thanks for telling me this, you all just motivated me to want to work harder to graduate." I didn't have feelings about his family reactions towards me, because they didn't like me anyway. I loved them though, and showed up, even while I and my kids were getting mistreated. My husband's uncle never changed how he felt about my kids and me. He showed us love when the family turned against us.

When I continued going to school, my husband made it hard for me. It's like the more I educated my mind, the more things were getting clearer. My mind has expanded, and I figured out what it was that I wanted to do after I graduate. I thought my husband would have been happy for me. He didn't take me seriously, and he was beginning to fall in the trap—the trap of not believing in me. He started listening to others, and started cheating on me with someone at his job. I still didn't let that interfere with my goals, and I kept on going.

Now my kids are growing quickly. At age 10, my son is running away from home, and stealing with his friends, and getting in trouble with the law. My son was going in and out of group detention homes, and I expected my husband to man up and lead the house, *but he had no leadership in him*. I started to recognize his poor leadership as our kids became older.

In a way, it was like the smarter I became, the more immature he was getting. I had to step up to wear both the pants and the skirt in our family. My husband had no idea how damaging this has become to our little family. His family stayed "in our business," believing he was too good for me. I remember hearing them questioning him, asking, "Why are you with her?" saying this only because I didn't live like them…or I refused too. I was raised with love and respect, for everyone.

I felt like I was in this alone—and my husband was turning against me.

My 10-year-old son is in and out of group homes because his chosen behaviors lead him there. Sadly, he was receiving absolutely no disciple or guidelines from his father, Ricky—and these things are essential to raise children, especially boys—so they are law-abiding and turn out to be good citizens. I'm trying to keep my daughters safe while being a good example for them. Being a wife, mother and housekeeper and also going to school was hard. I fought through it, because I understood where I was going in life. My husband didn't like the fact that I'm changing right before his eyes, nor did his family. The family that I came to love is now my enemy, and the hate became noticeable. My husband and I are starting to argue and have a hell of a lot of disagreements. Our household was falling apart slowly but surely. I had come to the conclusion that I'm at war—and I didn't ask for this battle that was handed to me.

I continued in school, although it was tough with no support. My teachers were my biggest supporters, all three of them believed in me. I felt loved coming to school, to hear my teachers say, "You can do it!" At times, I felt like giving up, but I'm a firm believer in finishing what is started.

During that time my husband and I lived down the street from his mother. His mother had two minor-age sons living with her at that time. All her other kids were adults in their own homes and with their little families. I started to fade away from family events because the love wasn't the same. When I did attend family events I always stayed off to the side, as I was a good observer. I was blessed with that gift—I understood that my children and I were not welcomed. They hated me, and sadly my children took the wrath. My kids were excluded during holidays, Christmas being one of the major events in their lives, never receiving a gift. My husband's mother made sure that her other grandkids received gifts. My kids received gifts of lies, the No. 1 favorite line of lies they told my kids were, "I'll get you guys something after Christmas." I was heartbroken as were my children, and I felt so bad for them.

My children never received what his family promised them. My husband seemed to not care that his family was mistreating our children. He was blinded by his family's way of life. I thought hard and long, asking myself if I made a mistake. My husband and his family had me questioning my loyalty to them.

Remember this is important:

Always make sure *you love yourself first and foremost,* so the scale doesn't tip—and someone else has control over you and your life.

CHAPTER 14
WEARING A DIFFERENT HEART

God is love. – John 4:8

I'm a person like this: Once I come to love such a person, I take it to heart. I was also learning that all people don't wear the same heart. As I was walking around with my head cut off, trying to hold things together for our family, I found myself slipping in school, not having enough energy to go forward. My mind is clouded with drama, feeling trapped with no one to turn to. I sat in my house depressed for days, crying, and avoiding my children. My husband was always out with his friends, so I felt like he forgot about us.

The way my husband was acting had become normal to him. It hurt me so much that I started praying, and I got down on my knees and asked God for strength. My prayers weren't answered overnight, but it came unexpectedly. One early Monday morning, a feeling came over me—a feeling out of the ordinary, and my heart felt heavy with butterflies in my stomach. A sudden boldness of courage entered my body. The dark place in my life became bright again, and from there, I knew my passion. I went back to school, only this time I was more focused. My teachers were excited to see me, and I was excited to see them, too.

My kids and my education played a huge role in my life. I knew I had to finish school for my kids. Even though we were a two-parent household, I was the only one changing while my husband remained the same. I became so frustrated because I had a lot on my plate—feeling like a single parent, but with a husband. With nobody to talk to, I used school for my peaceful place. Determined to get my GED, I started getting more engaged, paying more attention, and studying more at home. With all my hard work and studies, it paid off. I finally earned my GED, but I couldn't have done this without the support of my teachers. They played a big part in my life, and I was grateful for them.

After I received my GED on November 13, 2008, my future looked bright. I decided I wanted to go to college. My dream was to become a business owner, so I pursued my career in business management. The school of choice was The Minnesota School of Business/Globe University. I preferred night school only because of my kids' school schedule. They have school in the morning and I have class at night. It worked out great. Although my husband was working and maintaining his job, our marriage was still on ice.

I let nothing bother me, as I continued to stay focused. Two months after I received my GED, it was time to walk across the stage. I was already in college before I received my cap and gown. I was asked to write a speech for graduation day.

On the day of graduation, I read my speech in front of the other graduates and teachers. I was so happy that it took some time for me to read it because I was in tears, tears of joy. I was happiest seeing my kids watch me accomplish one of my goals. After all that excitement was over, it was time for me to get to work.

I signed up for Business Management, only to change my career when I decided to pursue music instead. I remembered that I came from a family of musicians.

I was told that my grandparents on my mother's side had over 20 children. All my uncles played different instruments, while my mother and aunts sang. My mother was the head singer, of course. They created a gospel band called the Barnetts. In my mind I'm following suit. I was excited to be in the music business, and I was learning a lot about the industry. I started teaming up with classmates, learning how to be comfortable talking on the radio. In class, we had DJ booths, and when I heard myself say it, it sounded weird.

I hated hearing my voice, but it was a part of our grade. Shortly after, I worked at a radio station as an intern. When I met with female radio personalities, I felt like I was finally a part of something big. My life started to shift for the better when I teamed up with a popular Minnesota rap group, and started to book hip-hop local events at popular venues.

My husband's family didn't like the fact that I was starting to shine. I had nothing but negativity coming from some of them. Their negativity didn't hold me back, I kept on living—and Ricky kept on cheating. The fact that I had important people coming to my house, picking me up for events, caused my husband to get jealous. He started to show his hateful ways toward me, trying to figure out how to hold me back. I worked hard to be in the position that I was.

I had dreams to move to Atlanta, Georgia, after I graduated from college. Now I have been in school for nine months, our assignment was to book a venue. I teamed up with classmates, and we had to find local performers for our show. We found a venue called First Avenue in downtown Minneapolis. I hired two performers, one being my husband's little brother who was into music. The other performer was his partner. I was excited because they agreed to perform for me. We locked in the date and time of the event. Three weeks before the spring event, it was a peaceful night in my household, but all of a sudden, we heard emergency personnel. They were speeding down the street, onto the next block where my husband's mother lived.

My big brother, who had been outside on the porch, now walked in and said to my husband that ambulances and police officers are in front of your mother's house. My husband was playing his game, so he didn't think anything of it. I asked him where his little brother was, but before he could answer, the phone rings. It was his other little brother screaming and crying saying, "Our brother has been shot." We rushed down the block to his mother's house, to find my husband's brother laying on the ground, across the street from his mother's house, fighting for his life. A few minutes later, he was pronounced dead on the scene. I felt so bad for his family, because I know how it feels to lose someone so close.

As his family grieved, I gave them space, and I went home to pray for God to give them strength. As time went on and the funeral was over, my show still had to go on. I had to find another performer to take the place of Ricky's brother. I asked my sister-in-law's boyfriend if he could perform, and he kindly said yes. He was also in a popular Minnesota music group that had a huge following. The day of the show arrived, people showed up, and the show was a success. I earned an A+, as well did my classmates. It has been a year since I've earned enough credits to transfer my credits to Georgia Tech.

CHAPTER 15
ON THE ROAD TO ATLANTA

I wanted to move to Atlanta, Georgia, to finish school—as Atlanta was the music capital. Everybody wanted to go there or live there, as it was wild, crazy, and fun. I finally came to the decision that I'm moving to Atlanta, and I felt like since I was on Section 8, I can find housing for cheap. The program helps low-income families, elderly persons, veterans and disabled individuals afford housing in the private market. After my husband agreed to the move, I told him I'm going to go first to find us housing. I'd take my youngest two with me, my oldest daughter stayed with her father for a few months, and my son stayed back with my husband. With my youngest daughters, ages 9 and 10, we left for Georgia on the Greyhound Bus. We arrived in Georgia the very next day. I called a cab and we ended up in Decatur, Georgia, at a hotel I knew nothing about. *All I knew was I had a dream to become successful.* An hour goes by, and I'm right around the corner from the Section 8 office, which was a blessing. I didn't know anything about Georgia. When I walked into the office, she had my paperwork on hand. When she looked up my name, my voucher was on her desk. Now it was up to me to find housing. I had my young daughters at my side—but I was running out of funds to pay for our hotel room.

I called my husband back in Minnesota, telling him I needed money to pay for my last night's hotel. He replied and laughed at the same time, saying, "Woman, come home." I was crushed by his response. He didn't care if we were on the streets. I stressed that I had no more money for the whole day. The next day came, and now it's checkout time at the hotel. I'm calling my husband for money. He's taking everything as a joke, now I'm worried because I'm in a different state with nowhere to go. My husband is literally giving me the run around—and disrespecting my needs, while I'm walking the streets of Atlanta with our two kids. He embarrassed me in front of his family. Everybody around him, including my family, made mockery of me. The rumors, the slander, and laughing, all because they wanted me to fail. Nobody in that circle offered a hand to me and my children. The day is going by so I rode the bus downtown Atlanta to see if I could find shelter for my kids and me.

We walked inside of the Atlanta's welfare office to seek help. I asked them if they have shelter for homeless families. I know people in my family and my husband's family were thinking…why doesn't she come back if she's struggling? Anyway, the worker found shelter for the girls and me. The shelter was on the other side of town, but I had no money to get there, and by this time I was exhausted. I could tell my daughters, age 9 and 10, were tired, because we had a rough day. With nobody to support us, not even my husband, I was confused and crying, wondering how could this be. Then this lady saw me crying. When she asked me if I was okay, I replied, "No!" I explained to her that I was new in Georgia, and was looking for housing.

This complete stranger asked me what area I was considering? I really didn't know because I was new to the state. A few minutes later, she asked me if I needed a ride somewhere? I answered, "Yes, I need a ride to the Atlanta shelter." We pull up to the shelter, I'm thinking that Atlanta has a good shelter — only to find out it's trashy. I had assumed that Minnesota and Atlanta were alike. Minnesota is a state that takes care of women and children, with no one left behind. Minnesota also has great shelters for men, practically a hotel room setup. Before she left us at the shelter, she gave me her phone number, and told me if we needed anything, to give her a call. As I walked away, I said, "Thank you." With a heavy heart, I'm sick that my mind is all over the place. I'm thinking that out of all people, how can my husband do this to us. I tried to call my husband, but he was too busy cheating with other women. He never answered the phone, now I'm really going through it. I tried to stay strong for my kids, but I knew they understood.

I didn't want to be in the shelter either, as it was very uncomfortable. Everyone had to sleep on the floor on a thin blanket. I refused to do so, so I called the stranger back. I told her my situation, and she heard my cry. In just 10 minutes, she was there to pick us up. She invited us to her three-bedroom house in Lithonia, Georgia. I felt a little relief, because now my kids can rest. She walks us to her guest bedroom, where the setup was nice and clean. My girls and I became comfortable, we took showers and went to sleep. The very next morning when the girls and I woke up, this lady had cooked breakfast for us. I thanked her, and we sat and ate. Soon after she started asking questions, asking me what my plans were. I told her my journey, my dreams, and goals. I also mention that I have a Section 8 voucher, and am looking for housing. She didn't know anything about Section 8, so she wanted more information about the program. We talked and chatted for a while, just getting to know each other better. Soon after, she invited us to stay with her, until I found housing.

I said to myself, "I know I need to believe in God" the way I'm staying at a person's house—and I didn't know her from a can of paint. My faith wouldn't let me give up…I kept on believing. I kept on believing that God had my back, despite what others thought about me. A few hours went by, and the lady came to me with an idea. Her idea was to become a landlord, she wanted to rent her house out to me. I think she knew it was a guaranteed payout. She decided to go to the Section 8 housing office to get information. She asked the woman at the front desk how she could get on the list for renters. The front-desk person gave her the list of acceptance. She went through the process for me. She finally was approved to put her house up for rent, through the Section 8 housing program, so the program was going to pay part of my rent, which was exciting. The very next day that lady took me to enroll my kids in school. I tried calling my husband again to tell him the good news, and he finally answered.

I told him I found housing so that he and my son can come soon. He says with a dry voice, "That's good." I'm really trying to understand my husband's behavior, because he doesn't seem happy at all. With nobody to talk to, I started talking to that lady. I was telling her about my husband and marriage.

Her advice was to leave him, because he's not supportive. I didn't take her advice because I loved my husband no matter what he was doing to me. I didn't believe in dividing families, especially mine.

Then suddenly the woman had a twist in emotions, all because I refused to give up on my family. She started to mistreat us, taking my money from me. I was receiving a SSI check for disability, and she robbed me blind. She decided she didn't want to rent to me anymore, and called the Section 8 office to do so. Now I'm really stressed, feeling like I was at square one.

After a month staying there, her reaction and pursuant action were very odd, very disturbing, which made me think that she must have been in a violent relationship—as a child or an adult. Perhaps how it ended bothered her to this day, and made her wish it turned out differently. Why else would she change so drastically—and without any thought, dump my little girls and me out onto the street.

I called back to Minnesota and reached one of my family members. When I told her what was going on, she informed me that one of my mother's sisters lives in Georgia. My cousin gave me my aunt's phone number, and I called her. When my aunt asked why I didn't get a hold of her sooner, my reply was, "I had *no idea* you lived here."

My daughters and I were sitting outside of the lady's house where we had been living for a whole month. I was glad to know I had family in Georgia. When my aunt asked me what my location was, I told her where we were, but she was at work so she couldn't pick us up. The woman's son volunteered to give us a ride to my aunt's house so I called her to say we were on our way, arriving at her house an hour later. I reunited with cousins that I haven't seen in years—since my mother's death. They were happy to see me as I was to see them. I took a deep breath and exhaled, because I knew my kids were going to be okay.

My cousins greeted me with open arms, especially when they found out we share the same dream as I did—the desire to invest their time in music. My family in Minnesota didn't understand the movement, which is why they were talking bad about me. I thought my Georgia family was great because they understood the assignment, they understood what it took to live out your dreams.

My husband and son are still in Minnesota, and my oldest daughter is with her dad. Once settled at my aunt's house, I started looking for housing again. My husband is running the streets of Minnesota, acting as if he doesn't have a family. I'm stressed, trying to hold everything together while moving around Atlanta. It's embarrassing to have a husband who is not giving us support. I still love him no matter what, even though I knew he was cheating. All the signs were plain—no phone calls, and he barely answered the phone. My husband and I haven't seen or touched each other in two months. It seemed like a year to me, and I missed him like never before.

Finally, I found housing in Duluth, Georgia. The house was a miniature mansion, but the owner did not accept Section 8; however, after he looked into the program, he signed up for the guaranteed income and was granted the license to rent. I called my husband and told him about the house. I had a little money, and booked flights for my son and husband to be with us. We stayed with my aunt and her kids for two weeks, until my house was Section 8 approved. My oldest daughter, who was with her father at that time, also came home. She was in Mississippi, so she wasn't too far away.

CHAPTER 16
THE FAMILY IS ALL TOGETHER

I'm happy we are now in our own home, and my four kids are in school. I was blessed to have my family together again. With my children being in school, and I have time on my hands, I signed up for Georgia Technical College, where I had my credits transferred. I felt like I could get projects done now as things seemed to be in order. My husband is looking for work, and I'm getting ready to attend school. However, I never made it to school because my husband's attitude started to change, and he started to give up hope. I decided to put my career on hold to help him find a job. He and I walked to the library every day to look at want ads while our kids were in school. We were determined to find him a job, but it seemed like no place was hiring.

I remembered one of my cousins' husbands was the manager at a restaurant. I reached out to him, and he advised my husband to put in an application. My husband didn't, and from that day, I knew he wasn't happy about the change. We started to struggle, and my husband seemed to not care. I was getting food stamps, but it wasn't enough. I was on Section 8, but paying low rent wasn't enough. Soon our lights, water and gas are disconnected. Because my husband wasn't willing to work, he made it really hard to live. He called his mother and family complaining about how bored he was, and about not having money for food. I felt that being the head of the household, he'd be stronger than this. His manhood showed weak signs by calling his mother, crying like a baby.

I was so frustrated at that point, because he couldn't man up. I started to take matters into my own hands. With so much chaos in our household, my children are out of control. My son is getting suspended, my oldest daughter is getting sent to school suspension. My youngest daughters didn't want to be in school.

My son, who was 12 years old at that time, decided to hitchhike back to Minnesota, and he made it all the way to Kentucky when I received a phone call. The Kentucky police transported my son back home.

Now it was so bad between my husband and me, and I was truly stressed because he had given up on us. We became distant from each other. Sometime later, my husband gets a phone call from his brother who excitedly told Ricky that his long-lost daughter is trying to contact him. My husband has two other kids from before we were married.

My husband is in tears because he hasn't seen her since she was three years old—and now she's 16. When he spoke with his daughter on the phone, he asked her where her mother was; she replied that she's deceased. My husband was shocked to hear the sad news; then she told him her mother had been murdered by her boyfriend when she was three years of age. When I spoke with her, I expressed my sadness for her because I knew how it felt to have your mother killed.

I haven't seen my husband this happy in a long time, especially since we moved to Georgia. A few days went by and Easter was right around the corner. Instead of my husband spending the holiday with us and his daughter in Georgia, his mother decided that she would pay for his plane ticket to Minnesota to be with her and the family. She also paid for his daughter's plane ticket so they can reunite. I wasn't upset because I knew what it was all about—it was about love and hate at the same time. My husband and his daughter are together with their family having Easter dinner. My kids and I are at my aunts. We had a good time, but I still missed my husband. He called me a few times, but not as often as I hoped he would.

Four days had gone by, and when Easter was over, my husband's daughter returned home to her grandmother who has been raising her since her mother was killed.

After the holiday is over and things are calming down, my husband is still in Minnesota—and not answering my phone calls. Already stressed, I'm thinking the worst of everything, like he was hurt and is in the hospital. I called the police station to see if he'd been arrested. I was doing everything in my power not to think that my husband was lying, and was with another woman. All the signs were there, but I didn't want to believe it. My husband's actions proved he didn't want to come back. I fell into deep depression, not wanting to cook and clean—so depressed that my menstrual cycle faded away. During the month my husband was absent, one of my relatives contacted me, saying that she wanted to move somewhere different.

I invited her to live with us, because I was lonely. My husband was out there cheating. When my relative arrived in Georgia, I was somewhat happy because I had someone to vent to. Talking to her about my relationship felt good as it was all positive energy. After the conversation, I was more motivated to get up. Now it's been almost three months, and my husband is still not with us.

One day it hit me, I knew I had to step in to do something and quickly. I contacted one of my friends in Minnesota, and I asked her for a loan. She kindly wired me money, so I went online and booked a flight to Minnesota. Since it was my first time booking a plane ticket, I booked one with a layover. I didn't know anything about it as this was my first flight. I called my cousin for a ride to the airport. I went to the gate not knowing what to expect; soon we started to board. Taking my assigned seat, we started to lift off, and I'm scared out of my mind— thinking crazy, like this plane is about to fall. The person next to me was laughing at my fear, but I really didn't think it was funny at that time.

As the plane descended, I feel a little more comfortable, and was relaxed, at least until the plane started to land. I asked the person next to me why we were landing, and he replied that we have a layover in Cleveland, Ohio. I was scared to a point that when the plane landed in Cleveland, I left the plane and went outside to smoke a cigarette, thinking I had time to calm my nerves, but when I came back inside, I discovered my plane has left after a 45-minute layover before heading for Minnesota. I was so upset, because I had to wait three hours before the next plane. After that long day of being confused, I arrived at the airport in Minnesota. I was glad when my husband and brother come to get me, and my husband acted like he was happy to see me. His approach felt a little off, in my heart I knew he was cheating. I didn't care about the fact he was cheating because I was just happy to be in his arms. My relative who was staying at my house in Georgia took care of my kids while I was gone.

When we went over to his mother's house, they thought they had seen a ghost, the way all eyes were on me. They couldn't believe that I was in town. I only came into town to bring my husband home, because he seemed to have become lost. We didn't go to Atlanta right away, because of our money situation. I had to wait until I received my SSI check to pay for our Greyhound tickets back to Georgia.

As we were getting ready to go back home, a tragedy occurred in his family.

His brother-in-law was fatally shot in the head; then his body was set on fire. It was another sad day for his family. I felt sorry for my husband's sister who had lost her high school sweetheart—and the father of her two boys. We stayed for the funeral, and shortly after we were on our way back home, arriving at the bus station in Atlanta, Georgia. Taking a taxi home, our children were excited and happy to see us. My husband and I are getting along fine, as he seems to be more at ease here.

My relative found her own home and had moved out. Because my family and I are together again, I was so happy that I made phone calls to Georgia Tech, wanting to get back into school. I've wasted too much time and energy to stop now. I thought with my husband being back home with us, I could focus on my career. Sadly, it didn't work out that way. My husband gets a phone call from his friend from Minnesota who asked what our address was. I'm shocked to hear that his friend is in town. My husband claimed that his friend was here to purchase a car. I went along with it, because I figured my husband had no reason to lie.

The friend was happy and ended up buying the car he wanted, so he and my husband went to celebrate and have drinks. I didn't mind because I knew the friend was going to be here for only a couple of days. My husband's attitude started to change again. The closer it was to his friend's departure, my husband started to get anxious. The car his friend had purchased was getting shipped to Minnesota from Georgia. His friend took a taxi from our house, and I thought they said their goodbyes. My husband was being so sneaky with his friend—then I found out the very next day that my husband had a plane ticket back to Minnesota. I was so hurt and confused that he had the audacity to have his friend sneak out and buy him a ticket.

Now I'm pissed off, knowing that my husband is about to leave us again. Because this was his plan all along, I felt so disgusted after all the things we've been through, but he still didn't seem to get it. I started to yell and cry, asking him why. He said nothing, I was so angry I threw a shoe at him. We started to fight, because he was leaving. I felt like my world was over. My husband left us—and his family was happy that he did. They wanted him to leave me, they wanted to prove me wrong. They knew I loved my husband, and they knew I'd do anything for him. They knew I wasn't going to give up on my marriage, it wasn't going to be that easy.

Life was so hard for me at that time, while my husband was in Minnesota living his best life. Everything went downhill from there, and I was stuck in Georgia. Thankfully my cousin was there to help me out. I was behind on rent, so my landlord filed for an eviction. I couldn't pay my water or gas bill. When the sheriff served me the eviction papers, I wanted to leave that day, but I was out of money, and didn't have a way back to Minnesota.

I called my husband to inform him I was served eviction papers, and I have court date. He chuckled like he was happy to hear the awful news, but it wasn't funny to me. I could hear his family chatting in the background. I'm telling my husband I have to be in court in four days. He boldly said, "I'll see you when you get back." *I burst out in tears because the man I knew and loved is no more.* Those days of waiting felt like four years of torture. Court date is finally here, and it was my turn to stand in front of the judge. The judge ruled in the owner's favor, which I didn't care about. I lost my housing voucher in the mix of all this drama. The judge had given me three days to be completely moved out. Thank God, because pay day was the next day. I woke up the next morning looking to buy Greyhound bus tickets for the kids and me. The tickets were more than what was expected, and I was $40 short for bus fare. The only thing I had of value was a

55" TV set that I sold to the pawn shop for $150. I'm still short, so I called my aunt in Minnesota. I told her I was short on money, and she wired me the rest.

The same day I was able to purchase tickets for us. I certainly appreciated my aunt because I was going through a tough time. I phoned my husband sometime later, hoping he would answer. My heart was beating so fast, and my stomach filled with butterflies. I was expecting the worst, because he's been doing nothing but disappointing me. Surprisingly, when he answers, I hear loud music in the background, with people laughing and chatting. Asking my husband where he was, he replied "I'm in Detroit." "Detroit?" I replied in surprise, and he answered yes.

My husband was comfortable at his family reunion, while the kids and I were sadly and emotionally stressed. From that day forward, I knew my husband and I were on thin ice. I cried as I packed the few things we had. Thankfully I had enough money left over for a cab ride to the bus station, and soon we were off to Minnesota. My children are happy, because they knew we were moving back. I had no idea where we were going to be living. I hadn't thought about it, all I thought about was my husband.

Halfway to Minnesota, I contacted my husband and told him our arrival time. He and my aunt came together to pick us up. I was happy to see my husband as we've been together for around 12 years at that time. I greeted my aunt with love, and she invited us to stay at her house for a while. I looked at my husband differently from that day forward. He had taken us back to square one as I was shaking my head from being embarrassed. I felt like I was back in the hands of my fellow enemies. My husband did not have a job. We're living off other people, sleeping on their couch, asking for rides because we didn't have a car. I had to start all over again, and not having Section 8 public housing, it was difficult for the owners to rent to us. We didn't have enough income to meet the owner's requirements. It was a nightmare, and since we moved back, we've been having bad luck.

My career was on hold, everything I've worked so hard for was now a memory. We lived from house to house, and it seemed my kids are going to different schools every other month.

I couldn't find housing fast enough, which made me so depressed. Luckily my oldest daughter's father was stable enough to keep her and my son—the kid who ran away to the streets, and did not listen to me. I was so tired of living and depending on people, and bouncing from house to house. It was harder, because we had no car. I told my husband, "As soon as I get my first-of-the-month check, I am going to buy myself a car." Buying a car was the best decision I could have made because it took a lot of stress off of me. Finally, my husband suggested we stay with his mother. I didn't want to, but it was better than sleeping from couch to couch. We didn't have our own room, so we slept in the closet of his mother's hallway. I was so embarrassed, because I had a husband who couldn't stand up as a man.

I've became tired of his family talking behind my back. I've put up with all the drama because I was bound. I've stood under God and made a vow to my husband, for better or worse and until death do us part. I took my vows seriously because I knew what it meant to be a wife.

I loved my husband more than I loved myself, and I'd do or accept what he did or wanted. I think I did this for our children—because having an intact family was important to me.

The mental abuse caused by him and his family was overwhelming. I had family on the other side of town, and I could have easily lived with them—but I chose to stay with my husband, no matter what he was doing to me. His mother and I couldn't see eye-to-eye; I truly couldn't understand why she hated me so much. I gave his mother the utmost respect, no matter how awful she was towards me. I remember one incident where she tried to throw gasoline on me; thank God she missed. She started to fight with my husband, because he disagreed with her. He thought she was going too far, so we ended up outside where she's making a big scene. The police were called, and she was arrested—for being intoxicated, and not listening to the police.

I wasn't happy in my marriage, and haven't been in a long time. Many times I wanted to pack up and leave, but my children needed me. They were sleeping in their grandma's warm home. My husband started to betray me, I felt like I was sleeping with the enemy. I came to the conclusion: he's never going to change. I slept in my car on cold winter nights to avoid the drama. I imagined myself "camping," as my husband joined me. It was so cold outside we needed to put a space heater in the car for warmth. My husband and I slept in the car the whole winter. I knew my husband didn't have to sleep outside with me, but I guess he knew it was one of the right things to do. We were struggling so badly, and his family blamed me for not having housing and money. His family would have meetings about me, talking among each other, always putting me down. I'm thinking to myself, "Are they unaware that my husband is their son, nephew and brother. I think they have forgotten about what a man is supposed to do to take care of his family. He was raised with no spine; it seems his mother raised him to be weak. I relied on my husband to be the best he could to me."

It is now spring, and we finally landed a spot in his mother's basement. I really hated it because of the spider webs as I despise bugs. The basement kept a damp smell, which was so intense it became the smell in my clothing. My husband didn't seem to mind living this way.

I paid his mother rent to stay in her house, as I always have. With my one-person income from Supplemental Security Income (SSI), it was hard to save money. I wanted to move out as bad as she wanted me to move. I could never save money because I was always reaching out my hand to help them. After I went broke from helping them, the attitude started up again. They loved me as long as I was doing what they wanted of me.

I was tired of sitting around with them, so I called one of my friends from school. She inspired me to get back into music, which sounded good to my ears—and I did just that. The very next day my friend called to tell me about an event coming up. The event was major, with mainstream entertainers, and they were looking for promoters. My friend and I took on the position, and it was uphill from there. She always came by to get me out of the house because I didn't look happy, and she knew I was depressed.

It is 2015, and the music industry is on fire, and everybody wants to be a rapper or singer. Because my friend and I are deep into this now, we started meeting all the major superstars. I had the pleasure of meeting one of my favorite rap stars out of Atlanta. That was huge, and we started getting invites to the best celebrities' after-parties, and were given VIP treatment. Unhappy and confused in my personal life, I still kept on pushing. My husband and his family are in a state of shock, because I wasn't bothered as much about their negativity.

My husband and his family felt pressured, because I've become popular. I started my own record label, called *Hambabyent*. I had thousands of followers on social media. Local rap artists were reaching out to me because they knew I was on to something. I became close with a mainstream rapper while living at my mother-in-law's house. When he came over, all their jaws dropped to the floor. They were sick to the stomach with hate, but I still remained humble. I understood my husband's family wasn't going to support me, because they didn't want to see me doing good or better than them. I was promoting and traveling out-of-state, doing big things in the music industry. My husband became jealous, accusing me of cheating with other men. However, all the time that he was the cheater, he assumed I was cheating because of the work I did, which involved all men. I had no intentions of cheating as I wasn't a groupie.

My goal was to finish what I've started—but my husband had a problem with it. I finally had enough money saved up for housing, because I was getting paid for promotion. After a month, I found housing, thinking I escaped them; however, we just moved to a house behind his mother, but I didn't care because it was my own home. I was finally out of his mother's house. His mother didn't like the fact that we had moved out, as she wanted to keep control. We moved into our house with nothing but a mattress. Sometimes, his family handed down "trash" they didn't want. I knew they thought of me as trash, and I didn't care because I didn't have to deal with them.

Living behind my mother-in-law was worse than living with her, and I never ever had a break. My husband started to hang with guys way younger than him, stealing clothing from shopping malls, and then selling stolen items. I hated the fact that he was stealing, but his family thought it was a cool thing to do. They used to put together a list of things they wanted for my husband, his friends and little brother to steal. I thought they were really insane, but that's how Ricky's family lived their life— by selling and buying stolen goods.

I'm not saying I was perfect, *but I had sense enough to know what not to do.* The stealing had become so bad that when our 16-year-old daughter also started stealing, I was quite upset. She started to believe that she would not go to school if she didn't have the latest fashion. My family fell apart by my husband's action, and with his family's help. She failed all her classes—but she didn't care—and her father didn't either.

Our other daughter, who was 14, started acting out and running away from home, because she feels mistreated by her father—that he was treating her sister better. She was witnessing her father steal clothes, but not getting her anything. She felt like her sister had more than she did, as far as clothes and shoes to wear to school. I felt so bad because I had only enough money for rent and bills. He didn't steal anything for me either. We looked like bums compared to those two.

One day when we weren't at home, my 14-year-old breaks in our house by climbing through her bedroom window. She knew her father had new clothing that he stole from the mall, and she took it upon herself to take some of her father's things and sell them. She felt left out, so she acted out. When my husband found out that some of his belongings were missing, he instantly gets upset when he knew that our 14-year-old had taken them.

Soon after we tracked her down at her boyfriend's. We knock at the door, and when the boyfriend's mother answers the door, we asked if she was there. The woman gave us a hard time—because she was reaping the benefits. I found out my daughter was stealing food from our house and taking it to her boyfriend's house. We had a big fight that day because my daughter was being disrespectful to us. One day, she and her older sister were fist fighting. I had to calm the situation down because I didn't like seeing my daughters fight with each other—they weren't raised that way.

After all that, the next day child protection came knocking at my door and questions me about the incident that took place a day before. My 14-year-old daughter had accused us of child abuse. They took her into placement, and she remained out of our home for several months. My husband and I were arrested sometime later, falsely accused of child abuse. My husband was working at that time, and he was fired for the child-abuse accusation. Our daughter took it way too far, causing harm, but didn't know how serious the situation was. Although our daughter was out of the home, we still had visitation rights.

Sometime later, child protection services (CPS) contacted us, suggesting our daughter be placed somewhere else. She thought it'll be a good fit if she's placed with family, so one of her aunts took her in. I was so out of place during these times when my marriage was on ice. My husband's family influenced him and made him believe our daughter caused all the mischief that had occurred. The things going on between my husband and me were not even close to what they were saying about our daughter. The problems my husband and I had, started way before the incident with our 14-year-old.

As our family was being divided, I was losing interest in my marriage but still I never left. I held on no matter what was going on. In my thoughts I just knew my husband would change for the better. However, there was no change in him, and he never took a second to think twice about us.

CHAPTER 17
INTO THE MUSIC PROMOTION BUSINESS

Three months have gone by and now it's 2016.

Our living situation has sprung out of control, my husband and I are not on the same page and haven't been in a long time, since he left me in Georgia. Not only was his mother living across the alley from us, he allowed one of his siblings to live with us. I agreed to let her stay because I loved my husband, and I didn't want to have an argument. Even though I agreed with my words, I wasn't agreeing in my heart because I knew it was a bad idea.

With all the chaos and commotion going on, I still managed to stay focused on promoting music acts. Although his mother and aunts had doubts about me and always put me down, I gave them a night to remember when I introduced them to a legendary artist and songwriter—someone they thought they would have never met in a million years. However, it didn't change how they felt about me.

A few weeks later, I was contacted by an artist manager. He had an entertainment business, and had managed my husband's brother before his death. He also had his own nephew as a rap artist. His record label was "Tony Cordell, LLC."

Tony Cordell contacted me on my social media Instagram page and asked if I could manage his nephew, who goes by the name T. Anderson. It had taken me a couple of days to give him a solid answer. The next time I spoke with Tony Cordell, I agreed to become T. Anderson's manager. That very next day was Ricky and my anniversary of 14 years of marriage. I invited Tony Cordell and T. Anderson to join us, so we could get to know each other better. They pulled up in a Hummer, shrink wrapped with T. Anderson's picture—and where to find him on all social media platforms. My husband, oh my, I've never seen so much hate on a person's face, but I forgot who I was dealing with. Tony, T. Anderson and I chatted for a minute about the project I had coming up, but of course the conversation didn't last long because I had to entertain the rest of my guests. Our anniversary party was a success and we looked good, but in fact, my husband and I were a mess.

A couple days later, Tony Cordell called and wanted to set up a meeting, so I agreed. I met with him over lunch, and contracts were signed. I felt so amazed because I wondered, out of all people, "Why me?" I think this was God's way of showing up at the right time. All I knew was that my candles were lit up again. I was able to have the Hummer in my possession, where I did marketing. I also hooked up with a makeup artist, so I really thought that I was living the life. She did my make up for every event that I had going on.

I was riding through the neighborhood in a Hummer promoting my artist. I put him on a level where he opened up a show for a mainstream R&B singer and songwriter. T. Anderson became popular overnight, although he already had a big social media following. I still "put the icing on the cake," and with my help, he was making noise. My record label was beginning to grow, it became popular among all Minnesota local promoters. We were getting invited to major parties. I tried to bring my husband along, but he would always assume that I was sleeping with one of the promoters. The way I thought, I don't have to sleep with anyone to get to the top. I'm better than that—I went to school for this.

I was always uncomfortable doing business when my husband was around because he would make it known how insecure he was. It was so embarrassing when I had to focus on his feelings. He made everything hard for me. Although I knew that my husband was wrong in many ways, I still tried to find the good in him.

My rap artist was taking off, so we started to get booked for radio interviews. T. Anderson even was booked to model clothing in a major online magazine. It was so cool to see great progress. Being an artist manager is hard work, made harder because I was dealing with a broken home at the same time.

My husband accused me of cheating so much that I wanted to quit managing. It seems that I always found a way to put his feelings before mine—and put my life on hold for him, and every time I did, it wasn't good. I was more depressed and fighting through it at the same time. My love for Ricky, whom I grew up with, was slowly fading away. I didn't want to be around his negative energy any longer, nor his family. My husband had toxic traits and learned behavior. Two weeks later my husband and I were served an eviction notice to vacate our home. We've been homeless off and on for six years, after we moved from Georgia. At this point I'm fed up, it's like, "Here I go again," so we ended up moving into my daughter's old apartment.

My husband became a poor excuse for a man. I think he had forgotten he was raising girls, and as a father, he should never want his daughters to date a man like him. I believe in some cases that fathers are the first ones who will give their daughters their first heartbreak. That's true, because I've witnessed it.

Meanwhile, I had a business to run. I was under contract, so I had to make things happen. Although I was low on money, I was able to do things that an average broke person couldn't do. Shortly after, I heard about a celebrity reunion tour that was being held in Atlanta. I thought that would be a great opportunity to promote my artist, T. Anderson. Instantly I called Tony Cordell to tell him about the tour in Atlanta. I suggested that it would be good marketing if I were to drive the Hummer to Atlanta. He agreed, because the Hummer was shrink-wrapped with T. Anderson's face all over it. Soon after, I made a phone call to my makeup artist and asked her if she wanted to go to Atlanta with me. She said yes, because she'll be promoting herself as a makeup artist. I talked with my husband about the tour, and he quickly agreed that I would go. His response seemed odd to me, but I had things to do.

A couple of days later, I went to pick up the Hummer. I talked with Tony Cordell for a second, he handed me the keys and I was on my way. I pulled up in front of my husband's sister's house where everybody was standing outside. They knew it was me, and they became envious. A few hours later my makeup artist met up with me, and it was time for us to hit the road to Atlanta. I said my goodbyes, I gave my husband and kids a kiss before I left. I was leaving for only a few days anyways. We arrived in Atlanta, Georgia, the very next day after long hours of driving. We drove around looking for hotels, but we had no luck. I called my cousin who lived 20 minutes from where we were. We went to her house where we changed clothes, got dolled up, and went on our way.

That night the streets of Atlanta were lit up like Hollywood. We drove to the arena where the tour was being held, and as we were driving by, I can see people stop to stare at the Hummer, wondering who is in it. They never expected two females to step out, but that's what they saw—US! As we continued to get all the attention, I kind of forgot what was going on in my personal life. We entered the arena, had a great time, but soon it was over. We stayed in downtown Atlanta for a while. As we were leaving, someone yelled out that a mainstream celebrity artist will be at this certain club. My makeup artist and I went to the spot they mentioned. Marketing and promoting was my mission. We had fun in the parking lot, as it seemed like the party was outside. Everybody was surrounding us—the Hummer was the main attraction. It gave us a good look, two beautiful females handling business from Minnesota.

We were out all night until about 6:00 a.m. At this point, we were tired so we drove back to my cousin's house. We slept all day; then we had to get up and do it all over again. Before we left my cousin's house, I made a few phone calls back home—one to my husband and kids, and the other to Tony Cordell. I let them know I was okay, and I'll be home in a couple of days. I met up with a friend from home who was also an artist manage. We linked up, and we all went out that night in the Hummer. The venue that we were at had a live DJ spinning records. I had about a hundred of T. Anderson's CDs to hand out, so I paid the DJ to put T. Anderson's CDs in rotation. After he did just that, the crowd was feeling the music, and the night was a success. We left the club and went back to my cousin's house. He had a recording studio in his home, which I thought was pretty cool. We chatted for a minute, and then we all fell asleep. Things were going well because one of my missions was completed.

The next morning my husband calls me, yelling about his debit card. I forgot I had it—and he's yelling, "You better not spend my money!" I was hurt and had no intentions of doing so, even though I was broke. I asked my husband if I could get some money because I was out of town. Thinking he would have sent me some money, but was not surprised that he didn't. He made me drive to Western Union to wire his money to him. I was so embarrassed, because my makeup artist had to feed me. I appreciated her for it because she didn't have to do it. The next morning it was time for us to leave Atlanta, I didn't have gas money to get back. My makeup artist was doing so much for me at the time, so I didn't want to bother her. I knew not to ask my husband for money because he didn't care anyway.

I called Tony Cordell and told him my situation. He kindly sent me the money to drive the Hummer back home. When we arrived back in Minnesota, I pulled up in front of the house. My makeup artist walked to her car and left. I sat in the Hummer for a minute before I entered the house. I was so disgusted with my husband that I didn't want to be around him. I'm asking myself, "Why am I still with this man?" I walked in the house while my husband was asleep. I softly tapped him on the shoulder to wake him up because I didn't want to frighten him out of his sleep. He woke up and looked at me. Never once did he ask me how my trip was. I really didn't expect him to be happy for me as he's been acting shady the whole time.

The next morning, I was up early to prepare for my day. First, I phoned Tony Cordell to fill him in on the things that had taken place in Atlanta. We chatted for a minute, and then we decided to meet up later on that day. As I hung up the phone with Tony, my husband showed signs of jealousy. The vibe and energy between us was way off. Although I haven't forgotten about what he did and has been doing, I still was able to say, "Good Morning" to him with love, which a wife should do. He reacted as I thought he would have. He looked at me out of the corner of his eyes, and said "What's up." To spark conversation, I asked him what did he have planned for the day? He answered "I don't know yet," so I proceeded to tell him my plans. He wasn't happy with my plans, but he never is. I ignored his feelings to pay attention to mine. Our conversation was cut short, because he turned his back on me. After he walked to the bedroom to get dressed, he went towards the front door. He tells me he is going to his mom's house, and that's where he'll be. I replied, "Okay, I'll meet you over there after I do some networking and promoting." The door closed, and I began to get to work.

As an artist manager, I had to do a lot of networking. The networking had paid off because my artist was landing gigs. What's more exciting than when my phone started to ring off the hook. I had a VIP call from Atlanta wanting to book T. Anderson who had become a hit all over again. During the phone calls, I was able to book a venue for the showcase I had in mind. With T. Anderson being my artist, he was the main attraction. I got in touch with Tony Cordell and told him about the vision I had in mind for the showcase. He understood the assignment. I figured T. Anderson needed a live personal DJ. Being in the music business, I knew of one who was popular in the industry. I reached him, and he agreed to DJ at the event. Now that's done, but I need an online flier design—one that stands out with T. Anderson's photo, date and time of the event. I knew who to contact, so I emailed him and we chatted. After I told him my vision for the flier, he asked for a photo of T. Anderson. I sent him the photo of my choice, and he went to work on it. I was able to get a couple hours of sleep before I had to meet with Tony Cordell.

As soon as I woke up, I called my husband to see where he was, so I could see him before my meeting. He said he's at his mother's house, so I dressed for the day. I went outside, jumped in the Hummer and drove to see my husband. I pulled up to his mother's house, only to get the feeling that I was being talked about in a bad way. When I walked into her house to greet my husband, his family gave me this uncomfortable look. Although my husband and I were on bad terms, I still wanted to make peace. I wanted to have a clear head before my meeting with Tony Cordell. My husband and I talked for an hour, babbling back and forth and getting nowhere. I went silent for a second and told him I have to go. As I walked out of the front door, I could hear his family saying, "She's not for you." I paused with sadness, but I continued on my way. I called Tony Cordell to tell him that I should be there shortly. Before I entered the meeting, I had to clear my mind from the family drama.

In the business meeting with Tony Cordell and T. Anderson, I was explaining to them about the event, and what to expect related to the lineup of the show. I told them I had contacted several other local rap artists to be on the showcase. I needed to add them to the online flier, before it was complete. While that was in motion, I received a phone call from a promoter down in Atlanta, Georgia. He was having an event and invited T. Anderson to perform. As I took his offer, I asked the promoter for the date and time of the event. I hung up and I told Tony Cordell and T. Anderson the good news.

The date and time of the event was right on the mark, because I thought we were all free to go. We were planning to drive the shrink-wrapped Hummer to Atlanta. I was surprised by a phone call from my doctor, telling me that I have to get surgery. Surgery for what I asked? She told me the condition, so I had to stay back in Minnesota. I knew that my health was more important, so I told Tony Cordell and T. Anderson to go on without me. I was so upset that I couldn't go to Atlanta with them. The day of my surgery was the day they were leaving. While they were in Atlanta—I was in the hospital healing, networking, and promoting.

While I was in the hospital, my husband visited me every day. He would sometimes spend the night if he wasn't to be busy out stealing with his friends. The stealing became like a hobby for him and his friends. I disagreed with it all; I wanted to earn money the right way. My husband was so far gone that he wasn't seeing it any other way. It had come to a point where I stopped fussing and let him do what he wanted—and he continued to do just that. I had given up on us.

I stayed in touch with Tony Cordell and T. Anderson while they were in Atlanta. T. Anderson was being interviewed by well-known promoters out of Atlanta. They were so well known in Atlanta that in today's time, they are rich. It's always about who you know in this industry—and being at the right place at the right time. I was proud of them because they were working. My job was to make something happen, and I was doing so while recuperating.

Tony Cordell and T. Anderson remained busy as they stayed in Atlanta. The next day it was finally time for me to go home from the hospital. My husband picked me up, and I wanted to go straight home because I was still sore from surgery, and I knew I needed more rest. My husband detoured and ignored my wishes. That made me very upset, but I didn't stress the issue because I had to heal from my stitches. We ended up at his aunt's house.

He claimed he had to drop something off to her (which were stolen good). I held my head down, with my hand across my face, I shook my head with second-hand shame. Shortly after their transaction, he finally takes me home. He didn't stay, because he said he has things to do. I honored his decision and he left. During my process of healing, other promoters were reaching out to me. We had crossed each other's paths in the past, because I've done some work for them. I was invited to a hip-hop event.

They informed me that they have booked a mainstream rap artist, and wanted me to be a part of it. I couldn't turn that invite down because it was all VIP status.

Tony Cordell and T. Anderson were still working in Atlanta, and so I decided to take my husband to the event because I wanted to show him so he could understand that absolutely nothing was going on between me and the promoters—it's all business. When we arrived, I checked in for the VIP pass with my husband beside me. As we walked in, I was greeted with love. One of the promoters took ahold of my hand and walked me to my booth. I was amazed because he set up everything for me. I guess it was a welcome-back present, due to my absence from having surgery.

I appreciated their love and support, but my husband felt different. He hated the fact that his wife was getting attention from other new men—which wasn't the case at all as the promoter and I had been business partners before I became independent. The night is still young, but I'm very uncomfortable. My husband is in VIP section with me, but has this "look" on his face, so obvious that I was questioned by one of the promoters who asked, "What's up with your husband?" Do you know how embarrassing that was? I can tell you it was, so I shook my head and shrugged as he walked away towards my husband. My husband saw him approaching and gave him this, "Leave me alone look." The promoter walked up to him, trying to make my husband feel comfortable—letting him know he has nothing to worry about. He told my husband, "Man to man, your wife is solid. It's just business and appreciation from me to her." My husband still wasn't buying it, so I decided we should leave. While driving home, we started to argue. The argument escalated and bad things were said—*finally I was telling the truth*. My husband said things to me that I will never forget, things that almost caused a physical fight between us.

I had to calm myself down because I felt like I was about to explode. My anger turned into tears, and all I could do was cry. I felt like giving up, like everybody had turned against me. My children's lives were all over the place—much of it in a negative way. My life was in shambles. My husband, with his family's help, made sure it was. My loyalty to my husband kept me trapped, I didn't know how to walk away; however, walking away ran across my mind over a hundred times. I still couldn't find it in myself to do it. Although I was a nervous wreck and totally stressed out, I did have work to do. I didn't care what my husband thought. I did what made me happy.

A few days have passed, and Tony Cordell and T. Anderson are now back from Atlanta. When we talked upon their arrival, I told Tony that T. Anderson was invited to perform at the First Avenue nightclub here in Minneapolis. I told them not to get too comfortable, and to be ready. Earlier that day I told my husband I had an event to go to. I told him when, who was performing, and where it was taking place. He said he didn't care, and he didn't care to go. Later that day, I called Tony. We talked about what time to meet up at the event that started at 9:00 p.m. We had to arrive an hour earlier for a sound check. Tony, T. Anderson, and I met up while he did a sound check; then it was time for the show. Tony and I stood side by side, watching T. Anderson perform.

When Tony Cordell looked down at me, and I looked up at him, our eyes connected, and I saw a sparkle. He pulled me closer to his side, and the feeling that ran through my body was like no other. The feeling confused me for a second, in part of my mind I knew this wasn't right. I have a husband, I thought to myself. I love him for sure, but where did this feeling come from? *Did I really love my husband or did my love fade away?*

Whatever it was between Tony and me felt good—and I haven't felt this way in a long time while being with a man. After the show is over, Tony, T. Anderson, and I are parting ways, saying our goodbyes with hugs. On my way home I called my husband, but he didn't answer. I called him a few more times and still no answer. He wasn't home, didn't come home that night— not until early that morning. I didn't question where he had been because I was still thinking about Tony Cordell. I wasn't cheating physically, but I was mentally, and *it felt both wrong, and oh-so right.* At 7:00 a.m., my husband takes a shower and gets ready for bed, a sure sign of a cheater. All the many years that my husband

and I shared together are coming to an end. He is now asleep as I leave to meet up with the team.

Our team talked about our next move to make T. Anderson the next big thing. After we did some networking and huge amounts of paperwork, we had completed our work for the day and went to dinner. I was having so much fun because I felt like I was around people who thought I mattered. With my husband being distant towards me, it was only bringing Tony and me closer. Lord knows I had no intentions on leaving my husband. As a matter of fact, I never thought in a million years that I would. After having dinner with the team, I was on my way back home. I never stayed out all night, no matter the situation. Although Tony and I had a little thing going on, I stood firm as I still had a husband.

When I returned home around 8:00 that night, my husband was dressed to leave. He once again shows a bad attitude, just so I wouldn't question him. I already knew where he was going, and that he was up to no good. It bothered me, but not as much as I thought. He leaves me all alone in the house. He never took the time to pick up the phone to call me. I knew he was cheating with another woman, but I didn't know who yet. It made me wonder: *Am I wasting my time*? While I'm being loyal to him, he's out there embarrassing me. He was bringing other women to his family's house, and his disrespect was at its all-time high. *I was over it*. I was getting played the whole time, while people were laughing in my face. A few days go by and my husband and I are still at odds. I was fed up at this point. I figured now that my kids are older, it was time for me to leave. My two older kids were already adults and had their little family and own home. My younger two, ages 15 and 16, were living with other family members because I made sure they were in a good position before I put my mission into action. I was working on clearing my mind and felt ready to leave their dad.

All the years that Ricky and I shared together are coming to an end.

The following day, my stomach was filled with butterflies, but I knew it was time to make my escape. My husband had no clue, nor did his family. With him gone from the house, I tried one last time to contact him before I really decided that it was over. As I suspected, he didn't answer. Sadly, I hung up the phone with tears in my eyes, and my heart was so heavy that it felt like it was pumping out of my chest.

I built up the courage to give Tony Cordell a call. He invited me over, and from there, "my life changed." Nervously I gave Tony a hug as he invited me into his house. To my surprise, he was a bachelor, and wasn't in a relationship, which was a plus for me. He owned a two-bedroom townhouse where he lived. It was fully furnished, but it had no real feeling that anyone actually lived there. Tony and I didn't have sexual relations yet, because I was still married. We talked for a while; then went to sleep. Now that 24 hours have passed, my phone started to ring off the hook. It was my husband calling me again and again, but I didn't answer, because I needed my peace. I didn't want any disturbance as I heal myself and become stronger. Although I was at Tony Cordell's house, I was still emotionally attached to the idea of being married. I know, I know that makes me sound weak in my personal life, whereas I am strong and confident in my business.

This went on for about a month. Only my oldest daughter knew where I was, but I trusted her to keep my whereabouts a secret…and she did just that. Between my husband and his family, I didn't know who insulted me the worst. So many rumors were going on about me. My husband threw dirt on my name, saying I left him and the kids *for a woman*. On social media, they all were slandering me, and were upset with me—but it didn't matter anymore because my mind was made up: *I wanted to be free, free from drama.*

Now I was living at Tony's house. Even though my husband was throwing dirt on my name, I knew he was doing it out of anger. It was hard letting go, but I knew returning to him would set me back. I had to be strong. I've cried many days while at Tony's house, all by my lonely self. I was hurt, confused and weak in the knees because of the separation between my husband and me. I was in deep depression, not eating and losing weight. I never wanted to go outside, and I thought my world was over.

I was second guessing myself, wondering if I made a mistake by leaving. I was all over the place in life, but Tony noticed and stepped in to ease my mind. He and I started getting more intimate as time went on. With him, I was feeling more confident. He started to take me out of the house, for instance going to the movies or just a walk around the park. It felt so good to breathe a little as my heart was still filled with pain. My husband stopped calling—and I was officially living with Tony.

Things were going smoothly for a while, until my oldest daughter phoned, telling me my husband had a heart attack, and was in the hospital. This was about 5:00 a.m. I hopped out of bed and asked Tony if he could drop me off to see my husband—and the kids' dad who had a heart attack. In God's honor, it was my duty to look after him. He was still my husband, and I honored my vows, even though we were not together anymore.

Tony gave me a ride, and we soon arrived at the hospital. I walked into Ricky's room and bent down to kiss my husband on the forehead as he lay in the hospital bed, just as the doctors came in. They told me he needed emergency heart surgery. I was instantly in tears—this was news I didn't want to hear. They rolled him back to the operating room for about three hours of surgery. I prayed for him the whole time while he was in surgery; now he's in recovery. When his mother comes to visit soon after, she gives me this dirty look. I respectfully ignored her, she stayed for a while, and then she went home. I stayed with my kids' dad until he was discharged from the hospital. I made sure he was well enough, to leave the hospital before I left. The way he looked into my eyes, he knew that I wasn't there to stay.

At that point, our relationship was pretty much over. I called my ride and left. I cried so hard later because I never dreamed that our family would not be together. It took everything in me not to turn back. I thought about our children, I thought about all the right things, on how to make us work.

As I thought about protecting everyone else's feelings,
I had to stand strong to protect my own.

I had to ask myself: I had my share of "bad relationships," so why was I trusting Tony now? First, these words came to me: Honest, faithful, positive, trustworthy, caring, aware, cares for other's needs—and much more. While I was wallowing in my marriage misery, he was always willing to take me out to fun and cheerful places, like the zoo, picnics, etc., and we traveled together to places I enjoyed seeing, like Washington, D.C. And, *he always makes sure my needs are being met.*

Tony's parents were highly educated and involved in their communities, and both had served in the Army, and as the youngest of four kids, he lived in Germany with them. However, in his wild youth, Tony had been sexually active like lots of young men, from which he has two wonderful sons he is very proud of, and sees them often. A grandson is playing basketball of University of North Dakota. I did not have the honor of meeting his mother because she died before I met Tony, and his dad died in 2024. Tony has two sisters who I've enjoyed getting to know because they also have his caring personality. When we first met, he told me he had asked God that if he would send him a good woman, he promised to treat her right—and I am the one.

As I have become stronger since being away from Ricky, I started to come out more. I spent time with my two minor-age children, age 17 and 18. I could see the sadness in their eyes; I knew what they wanted. They were expecting us to reunite as a family. I took them out for lunch to explain that Mom and Dad are not together anymore—that our relationship is too far gone at this point. I also explained that I'm filing for a divorce. Their faces dropped and tears started to roll down their cheeks. I couldn't help but feel their pain, as I know it hurts. When lunch was over, I dropped them back where they were living with an aunt. I wanted to continue to be in contact with them. I didn't miss a beat making sure they were well taken care of. Although they were off balanced and confused, they kept it together. I was more at ease, during my transition.

Tony and I have been together for some time now. Finally, I was ready to file for divorce, and I followed all the necessary steps. I went down to the court house, and a date was set. A few days later my husband was served his divorce papers. He wasn't happy at all, and I knew he was mad, hurt and embarrassed. However, I have feelings, too. The closer the date became, the more I felt sick—like I was going to a funeral. In my lifetime, I wouldn't wish this feeling on anybody, not even my worst enemy. It's not a good feeling at all. My husband and I grew up together. He was 21 and I was 20 when we met. We've been together for 20 years, and I thought, in my heart, that we'll go 20 more years.

It is March 23, 2017, and sadly the day has come. I woke up early to prepare for this devastating day. As I showered, my heart was heavy as tears rolled down my face. I thought about this over a hundred times, asking myself, "Am I making the right decision?" My thoughts were not 100 percent whether I'd show up for divorce court. I almost didn't go, but by now, I was in too deep. Court starts at 10:30 a.m., and I arrived by 10:15. I'm crying my eyes out because I never wanted to be divorced.

With court now in session, the judge exits her chambers. Entering the court room, she looked around to see only me present. She walked to the bench and sat in her chair. She waited for my husband for about 10 minutes, to give him time to arrive. He never showed up, so the judge proceeded to go on without him. My husband finally shows up 20 minutes later as we were just wrapping up. The judge asked him, "Is there anything that you would like to say?" He replies to her saying, "Whatever Tamica said, I'm fine with it." I looked over at my soon-to-be ex-husband, who showed no emotion whatsoever. He came into court with pride, and didn't want to fight for our marriage. The judge gave us one last time to reconsider, before she gave her ruling. My soon to be ex-husband's mind was clearly made up. I'm pretty sure he was encouraged by some of his family members. It was time to sign papers, and Ricky was the first to approach the bench. We both signed the divorce papers.

He walked out the courtroom laughing, and I walked out crying. I felt like a part of me had died—while he was on social media bragging about our divorce. I was absolutely disgusted by his behavior, as I really thought he was a way better person than that. I sunk into depression for many days after my divorce, while my ex-husband is out there living his responsibility-free best life.

It finally came out who my ex-husband was dating. It was one of his sister's friends, and has been for six years while we were still together. I choked because that really bothered me, even though we were divorced. This woman had been in my face at family gatherings—only to see and be with my then-husband at that time. To me his behavior was so lowdown as a husband

and a man. For six years, he was living a double life, and his family knew it.

Our divorce was still fresh, and although I was living happily with Tony Cordell, I found myself being jealous because my ex was boldly dating other women. I believe he tried to make me feel that way by posting his activities on social media. It kind of worked because—I know it is weird—but I felt like I needed him back. I wanted to prove that I was more important than those other females.

During all my faults and disappearing acts from Tony's, he still stayed by my side. He never gave up on me, because he knew exactly what I was doing and going through. Tony, being the man that he is, patiently waited for me to get my ex-husband out of my system. I appreciated Tony because I had a lot on my plate. He could have easily given up on me because of the way I was treating him.

I knew Tony loved me because he showed it in many ways. I just didn't know how to correctly love him, because I never was loved correctly by anybody. I prayed to God for strength and healing, and was baptized in the name of Jesus Christ. Soon after, a feeling came over me for I knew God had heard my cry. *I started to understand what real love felt like—and Tony Cordell was it.* The strong feelings that I had for my husband have faded. I've become strong and confident enough to see my ex-husband and walk away.

Tony and I are closer than ever. I was comfortable enough to talk with him about getting my own apartment because I still had two minor children to care for. Tony thought that was a wise idea because my daughters needed their mother, so I moved into my own apartment, and Tony had his own.

After the girls and I were settled in our apartment, I'd go stay at Tony's house. I figured my daughters were well put, since they were already 17 and 18 years old at that time. I didn't need a babysitter. I had my teenage adult daughter watching over our home. I made sure they had food and toiletry and money as needed. While I'm at Tony's house, my ex-husband found out I had my own apartment. He tried to interfere in my life by calling our daughters, asking about our whereabouts. I guess he thought that since I had my own apartment, he would come over anytime he feels like it—just because I was at Tony Cordell's house. With our daughter living practically on their own, he thinks he can stop by whenever he pleases. I had to put a stop to that because I was in a fully-grown relationship. I had to let my ex-husband know that what he was doing was not acceptable. It had to come to an end because we are over. He wasn't happy with what he had heard. I really didn't care because he wasn't my problem anymore. Ricky was so upset that he turned our 18-year-old daughter against me, feeding her lies as she was still vulnerable from our divorce. He convinced her to pick a side between us, and she decided to be on his side.

Although my 18-year-old daughter was living with me, she became very disrespectful towards me. Her mouth became reckless, the words that she shouted were unbelievable. The name she called me hurt so bad. I never knew my daughter felt that way. The anger that I had in me towards her caused me not to want to be around her at that time. She was out of control. I forgave her because I knew my bitter ex-husband was the cause of all this. I knew that my daughter was still confused and hurt about our family breakup. This is why I was able to overlook her actions. My daughter remained in our home for quite some time afterwards. I would leave from Tony's house every other day to check up on my girls, and see if the apartment was in order and clean. As a parent I still had duties. I ended up staying at home for the night to be with my girls. We cooked together, and had a long talk over dinner. My 17-year-old daughter understood where I was coming from, while my 18-year-old wasn't even trying.

She and I have been clashing ever since my ex-husband had that conversation with her. I still had to be strong and move forward from her feelings. The next day I called Tony and asked if he could come and pick me up after he leaves work. He said yes, and when he picked me up, we went to dinner. We go back to his place, and when he explains that he is selling his townhome, I asked why. He said he is moving to Los Angeles, California, and asked me to go with, and I quickly said yes. Soon his house was sold and he booked his flight out to California. He stayed at my apartment for two days before his departure. I was sad because he had to go ahead of me to get housing. His son was already a resident of California so he quickly found housing for us.

When I told my daughters that I was going to California, they asked me who is going to stay with them when I leave. I haven't thought about that because one of them was at a legal age.

Coincidentally my oldest child called to tell me he and his wife have nowhere to go. I thought that was perfect timing. My son also had my granddaughter. I told him that I'm moving to California, and that his family can come live in my place and have my room. It was a three-bedroom so it worked out for them all. The same day that Tony booked my flight to California, my son, his wife and my granddaughter came over, and they brought little-to-nothing of personal belongings with them. That was all they needed anyway, because my place was fully furnished. I showed them to their room, with their own private bathroom included. My son and his wife were pleased. My granddaughter is who I thought about, her being comfortable and safe was my goal.

The day is almost over, and I'm exhausted, tired from packing, and exhilarated from playing with my granddaughter. At this point I'm winding down. I grabbed my comforter and slept on the couch that night. The next morning, I woke up my son and two daughters. I had a talk with them before my airport driver arrived. I laid down the rules of being responsible adults. They understood the assignment, and we all agreed. I gave them hugs and kisses, and I was on my way to the airport. Arriving there, I called Tony to tell him that I'm on my way, and what time I'll land.

I was glad he agreed because obviously he was very excited to see me. That felt so good coming from someone who cares for me. It's boarding time and I get to my assigned seat. I put my headphones on and up we go. Four hours later I landed in LAX. I have never been to California before so this was exciting. I went to baggage claim and wandered my way to the front entrance. Without me having to call Tony, as he was already there waiting for me. I felt like a little girl all over again as this man warms my heart. He gets out of the car and comes around to the other side. He grabs me by the waist, pulls me close to him. He hugs, he kisses me, and I just melted in his arms. I said to myself, "He is truly my man," no doubt. He took the luggage from my hands and placed them in the back seat. Leaving the airport, we drove through the city. My eyes became big and wide as we drove to Beverly Hills. It was a beautiful sight to see. I loved the fact that we were touring around, but it had to come to a stop.

I was ready to freshen up from the long flight, so Tony and I made our way towards home. We had an apartment downtown in Los Angeles. Our apartment wasn't that big but it was very expensive. I guess that's the price we have to pay to live in California. We didn't mind it though because it was only us. Later that day, we were ready to go out—it was time to hit Hollywood. What a view as we drove down Hollywood Boulevard. I saw so many animated characters as well as actors standing on the street corners dressed in costumes. My favorite was the Michael Jackson look-alike who knew all of the moves. It was so exciting to see that I couldn't believe I was here. We tired from driving around so we decided to park and walk a bit. The streets of Hollywood had so much action going on. On every corner it was a photoshoot. Being my first time in California, I wanted to do and see it all. We walked for about two hours until we worked up an appetite. So many restaurants lined the Boulevard that it was hard to choose one.

We finally found one that had grabbed our attention. The restaurant was surrounded with bright lights. Classical music was playing as we walked through the door. We were greeted and seated at our table. We ordered drinks and appetizers for starters. We stayed there for a few hours; then we ordered dinner to go and left for home.

The next morning Tony suggested we should sign up for acting school. My eyes became huge with excitement, I couldn't believe what I was hearing. I gave him a big hug and said let's do it. We went to North Hollywood where the acting classes took place. We signed up and we were learning to act, for a price of course. Soon after, we received information that a casting crew is looking for extras to film a movie. Tony and I quickly jumped on it. We drove to the location where we had to sign up. We filled out the paperwork; then they took multiple photos of us. A couple of days later the casting crew called, saying we were booked and would be paid to be an extra. I won't mention any of movies we were in because we were in so many.

Sometimes we would be on set together, rest of the time we worked alone. We had a ball filming with heavy hitters in entertainment. My favorite part was the wardrobe, hair and makeup. I felt like a celebrity at that moment. It's funny because I never thought I'd be an actor. It had never crossed my mind, but Tony brought the gift out of me. Things were going fine for us. I loved the fact that we matched each other's energy, plus we were both in the world of entertainment.

In between times I would call home to check on my kids, to see if they are keeping up with the apartment and other responsibilities. It seemed as though they were, until I received a phone call from the manager's office stating that a lot of "people traffic" was going in and out of my apartment. In frustration I called my son and told him what I heard. He told me it was only his friends that were coming over. I told him it was not okay for his friends to be at my house. I knew the friends that he hung around were up to no good—and I didn't want them in my apartment. I stressed to my son that I gave up my space for him and his family. I told him he needs to appreciate what I gave him for his family. He agreed as we hung up the phone. Two days later the apartment manager called again. My son is not following rules—and he's not keeping a low profile. I'm upset and angry because I now have to fly back to Minnesota. Shaking my head as I hung up the phone, I looked over at Tony who could tell something was wrong by the look I gave him. He asked, "What was wrong?" I replied in a soft, upset voice that I had to go back home to get things in order, hopefully staying for only for a couple of days.

Immediately Tony booked my flight to Minnesota. I was so disappointed in my adult children, because they couldn't hold it together and follow the rules. I found out my son and his friends were carrying guns around the apartment. I saw it with my own eyes, as he was dumb enough to post it on social media. At that very moment, I thought, "What an idiot." I phoned him right away, and I told him that I'm on my way back, and when I arrive, I will clean out the apartment. Angry, he hung up on me. My nose flared, and it felt like steam was coming out of the top of my head.

I turned to Tony to say that my son really doesn't get it. Tony had a sincere look that said, "Go home to care of your business." I said to myself, *without this man by my side, where on earth would I be. He is so supportive in every way that I can imagine.* An understanding guy like Tony Cordell is hard to come by, and I appreciated him with everything in me. Although I was upset about what was going on in Minnesota, Tony would always find a way to make me happy. Around noon the next day, I was on my flight back to Minnesota. I called an Uber ride after I landed. I made it to my house, but didn't have a key to get in, so I knocked on the door. As my son opened it, he looked like he had seen a ghost. He was surprised to see me, and before I could walk in the door, he starts an argument. Immediately I told him to step on the brakes. I asked him, "Who the hell do you think you're talking to like this?" I said with a loud voice, "I gave you and your family a nice place to live in—so for you to treat me like this is uncalled for." I persisted in telling him to grow up because he has a wife and a daughter to think about.

He didn't want to listen so he decided to move out. Sad but true, I didn't stop him. I thought about how hard it was for me to get this apartment. I wasn't going to jeopardize my livelihood for anybody. After that was over, I was still upset, and my girls heard me and came out of their rooms. I was waiting for them to say something to me. They knew I was upset so they waited a while until I calmed down.

Calling Tony in California, we talked for an hour. Afterwards, I left the couch and went to my daughters' rooms. I told them how disappointed I was in them, too. I explained to them that I shouldn't have had to come back—with you all being adults. They tried to point fingers at one another, but I just said to forget it. Talking to teenagers can be like talking to a brick wall. There was no convincing them, so I moved on from that conversation. Meanwhile, the apartment is finally coming together, after all the cleaning, rearranging, and getting things back in order.

My life is a little more calm, too calm for me actually, and I started missing Tony Cordell. I started to get lonely and anxious. I wanted to be with him, but we've only been apart for two days—those two days felt like two long years to me. I was desperate to be with him, but my daughters didn't know how to be responsible. I was calling Tony all day and every day for a week straight. All I could think about was how he held me at night, and the feeling of his heart as it beats next to mine. I have never ever felt so strongly about a man. He gave me butterflies, like no other. Sometimes I would call him, and he'd be with his son and nephew. I thought that was cool because he could stay busy. In addition to being with his son and nephew, he did other things, like acting, to kept him busy during the long days waiting for me to return. I know he was desperate to be with me too; however, I had to take care of issues at home.

Another week passes when my daughter's friend calls. When she asked, "Is your mother going back to LA?" my daughter asked her why she wanted to know? She said, "I want to rent out her apartment." My daughter tells her to hold on, while she talks to her mom. My daughter comes to me with the news. I thought it was a brilliant idea. She offered to pay all the bills, which couldn't get any better than that. I agreed, and she was now my new tenant.

When I phoned Tony with the news, he was happy to hear it. My daughter's friend seemed responsible, so I never second-guessed her. She'd move into the apartment. We talked, and I was on the next airplane going to California. *Peace of mind for once is all I wanted—and being with Tony as he was my peace.* I was so excited to see Tony I felt like a teenager, going on her first date. I soon arrived in California, and Tony was there on time as usual. He watched as I walked to the car; then he stepped out and hugged me so tightly. It took him a minute to realize I couldn't breathe so he had to let me go. He kissed me softly, and we left for home. Tony and I are back on track. I started acting again, and in our free time, we go to the beach, enjoy picnics and relax.

What I admired most about Tony was that he had ambition and drive. He's adventurous as I am, and his eyes were always on the prize. We are perfect for each other, because we share the same interests. As we started to spend more time with each other, I started to open up, telling him more about me. He does the same, from that day on I became all his.

After my divorce, plenty of men come out of the woodwork who wanted to get with me, including my ex-husband's friends, but I saw no other man but Tony.

Just as I thought that things were falling into place, my daughter called me to say, "Mom, the electricity was shut off." I was upset because I knew the outcome. With the electricity turned off, I had to return to Minnesota. I asked my daughter, "How did the lights get turned off?" because in fact, the bill was little-to-nothing to pay. My daughter couldn't give me a good enough reason, so I hung up the phone.

With that being said, I had to fly back to Minnesota to the rescue. I told Tony what had happened, and that I had to go back. His response was, "Go handle your business," as he always supported me. The next day when I returned to Minnesota, my daughter had friends over. She knew I was already upset so her friends quickly left my apartment. I told my daughter that she's not ready to be an adult. She tried to argue with me, and I told her I'm not about to go back and forth. When she storms off to her bedroom, I started to make calls. Thankfully, the state of Minnesota had resources for low-income families. They were able to pay my whole light bill; however, the electric company couldn't come out until the next day. My daughters were learning how to manage things—but each time they initially did it the "hard way."

I called Tony to tell him the good news, which he was happy to hear. Now with things in order, he asked me when I was planning on coming back. My response was that I'd decide in a couple of days. We talked for a while. I walked in my daughter's bedroom to inform her about the electric situation. She and her friend were excited about it. I told them that I'll be leaving in a couple of days, going back to California. They were happy to hear that. Later that day, it was dark when the sun set. With the electricity being off, there was no power. My daughter and her friend didn't want to stay in the dark. Selfishly they booked a hotel for that night, leaving me in the dark. I thought that was pretty bogus on their part. I came back only because they couldn't do it without me. That next morning, the electric company came and restored my service.

My daughter and her friend came back to the apartment — with their boyfriends. I thought that they were insane, coming back to my apartment with friends. I didn't appreciate the fact that they left and didn't care to see if I was okay or not, they only thought about themselves. I knew while I was out of state that my daughter and her friend had parties. My daughter's boyfriend and their friends were all in my apartment, maybe six or more at a time. I couldn't control what was going on while I was out of state. I didn't bother to think about it. I was the type of parent that if my daughters wanted to have boys over, they could never spend the night as long as I'm there. I refused to have people running in and out. I slept on the couch because my bedroom was rented out. My daughter and her friend disobeyed my rules. They continued to let their boyfriends and their friends in late nights. I couldn't sleep so I took action, I told their friends off. I told them that as long as I'm here, y'all can't come over. I didn't like the fact that they were walking around me while I was asleep. I told them this is still my place, and everyone needs to get out. My daughter and her friend became upset, but I didn't care. I told them to give me a couple of days, but they couldn't respect it. Both of them leave with their friends, going out the door full of an attitude. A couple hours later some of my cousins heard that I was in town. They came over and we chatted, I cooked tacos and we ate. I was having a blast until my daughter and her friend came back. My daughter approaches me in front of my company. She says that her friend wants to move out, and I said "Okay." I continued to entertain my company.

The next day comes, and my family leaves after spending the night with me. After I slept on the words that my daughter said to me, I called Tony with sad and bad news. I told him that I have to stay. When he asked why, I simply said that the renter wants to move out, and I didn't want to lose my housing. He agreed with my point, and we were both heartbroken as we knew this was going to be a long process for us to be together.

As I hung up the phone with Tony, my daughter and her friend approached me. I guess they heard the conversation between Tony and me. In a laughing manner, they told me that my daughter's friend had changed her mind. She decided she didn't want to move. I looked at both of them with a straight face and said it's too late. With my mind already made up, and knowing I had to step up, it was over for her, so I explained to her why. I told her that "I am a grown woman," and I don't take things lightly. When it comes to my livelihood and my personal peace, no one else's opinion matters. The roommate thought that I was joking, but she soon found out how serious I was. I gave her time to move out with her belongings. The lesson I taught her was don't "play with grown women."

My daughter was so upset because they were "partners in crime," but I didn't care. All I know is that I gave them fair warning. I had to stand on what I said, although my daughter was cursing me out. She even called my ex-husband, who is her father, to rat on me, saying things that weren't true. I laughed at him and her, saying, "This is my place, and neither of you pay my bills." I knew my ex-husband had it out for me anyway, because of our divorce. His job was to humiliate me at all costs. He was bitter and had hate towards me—*he shouldn't because he caused all of this.* I paid no mind to him or her because I was on a mission.

Soon after her friend had moved completely out, I had my place back. While Tony is in California, I had my own responsibilities. In order for me to keep my apartment up to par, I had to find a job. I started job searching and landed a good one on the bus line close to my apartment. It couldn't get any better than I thought. I called Tony to tell him that I found a job working in the food area at a major grocery store. He was excited for me and cheered me on. I worked hard, and best of all, I could use both my food preparation and my "people skills." My working hours were 6:00 a.m. to 2:00 p.m. I had good hours for my shift. Everything was going great, even though Tony and I weren't together. I had to be strong and understand that this was all temporary. Waking up alone and sleeping alone was the worst ever, for I wanted my Tony.

A long month had gone by, and both of my daughters were home with me. I was off work that day when my older daughter received good news. She was accepted for a one-bedroom apartment. I was happy for her because all she brought to me was drama during her stay in my place. She and my younger daughter started arguing, which was getting on my nerves. So now the day has come for her to move out. She's excited and so was I. It was her first apartment on her own. I made sure she had the things that she needed.

I called Tony to inform him about my daughter moving out. He was happy for her; he even sent me the money to buy her a few housewarming gifts. That was so sweet. Now with my 17-year-old daughter at home with me, she still had rules to follow living there. She had two rules to follow. One was to stay in school, and two, do her chores. I made it very simple for her. However, she couldn't follow my rules, so she moved out with her boyfriend, someone I've never met. She had kept him a secret because she knew I was going to judge. I wanted both girls to choose wisely on who they date. *Dating comes with pain—and relationships can bring bad consequences because of someone else's bad behavior.*

For a few weeks, my life was filled with just going to work and then back home. I was home alone, and living at peace. I was on the phone with Tony most of the time. My daughters would come over for dinner, after they'd found out what I was cooking. It was pretty cool, but I was missing Tony. After my daughters had dinner with me, and they left. I cleaned up the apartment and relaxed. When I called Tony before I went to sleep, we talked for about an hour.

That next morning, I went to work, and on my break, I called Tony. He told me the best news ever—he said that he's moving back. My heart felt like it was just floating with excitement. That news he told me while I was at work had me on cloud 9. It's only been a month and a half not being with him—but it felt like years. Tony told his son of his plan to move back to Minnesota, and his son took over the lease of Tony's apartment in California.

It all worked out perfectly in our favor, and my Tony was on his way home to me. I was smiling ear to ear, and I couldn't wait to hug and kiss him. Two days later Tony was home, arriving while I was at work. His best friend picked him up from the airport. Tony called me to get the keys to our apartment. They drove up and he came inside to where I was working. My eyes lit up as he walked towards me, seeing the sparkle in his eyes. I walked around the register and we tightly hugged each other. I didn't want to let him go, and he knew it. We finally released one another, and he looked down at me with a smile. I handed him the keys and as he walked away, he said, "I'll see you when you get off." Being anxious and excited to get home was an understatement. I had only two more hours left, but it felt like forever. I tried to stay focused but it wasn't working. Time wasn't moving fast enough for me…*I wanted my Tony Cordell.*

My shift is finally over at 2 p.m., and I clock out without saying one word to anybody. I was out in a flash, and I didn't even look back. The city bus that I took home, dropped me off right in front of my apartment. I took the elevator up to the third floor where I lived. When I knocked on the door, Tony let me in. I fell into his arms even before he could close the door all the way. He bent down to kiss me as I came inside. We did some catching up for a while, as couples do. We relaxed, freshened up and dressed for the night. We decided to go on a dinner date. He knew that I liked sushi, so he booked a nice Japanese restaurant. Our transportation was an Uber cab ride. Our two cars were still in California, but were being delivered to Minnesota. We had dinner and went back home. I didn't have to be at work the next day so we watched movies.

I was so happy to be with my Tony. I haven't felt his touch in a long time. At that very moment I realized that he really loved me because this man had patience with me. I had so much going on in my life that any other man would've left. I appreciate Tony because he changed my mindset. Having him around I felt free, I felt all women. I had help with bills. I didn't have to ask him. He was a standup guy, and I loved it. It felt so good not to wear both the pants and the skirt in a relationship. I was finally able to buy what I wanted. All I had to think about was half of the bills.

My kids were finally adults. In between times, both my oldest son and daughter were having kids. My son had two and my daughter had three. I was a grandmother of five in 2018, and my life was starting to settle.

CHAPTER 18
2019 – AN INTERESTING YEAR

Because Tony and I were happily working on our relationship, I could finally breathe. We had money saved up, and both cars were at home. We were inseparable—living nice, stepping out into town more, and he taught me how to love again. My ex-husband caused a lot of unknown damage. With his family's help, he lost a good woman. Tony became the apple of my eyes. I had been at a point of no return. Tony made me feel like a woman with no competition. This was the type of man I had wanted my ex-husband to be like—a man with class and ambition.

My mother always said, "You can't have two doors open, you have to shut one first." After I remembered what my momma said, I shut the door connecting to my ex-husband and his family. Then it felt like an enormous weight was off my shoulders, as those memories soon faded away. I understood that they are my past—*and Tony is my now*. It felt so good to be whole again.

I reached my kids and had all four of them come over. I found I liked to cook for them, even though they are adults. My five grandkids were present too, so we had a family reunion. I did this for four months straight, while working. Tony was there to help out. Those days were perfect, because Tony and my kids spent time getting to know each other a little better, and I felt more at peace.

CHAPTER 19
2020 WAS BOTH LIFE-CHANGING AND BITTERSWEET

It was election year, the pandemic came, and people were getting sick from COVID.

I was working at the time and so was Tony. Because he worked at a public school, he had to leave his job because of the pandemic. I stayed at my job for a few months because I worked at a grocery store. During that time, life started to get crazy.

People were leaving their jobs just to get unemployment. A lot of people with money were on unemployment. I wasn't worried at the time, until one of the employers at my job had COVID. I was working with him a day before he came in with his doctor's note. A couple days later I started to feel ill—my body was hurting, I had a slight headache, and my nose was clogged. I told Tony how I felt, and he suggested I go to the emergency room, and sure enough they said I have COVID.

I was scared out of my mind, but thank God my illness wasn't that severe. I went home soon after and called my job and informed them of my illness. I also told them I will not be returning to work. I became unemployed, and I filed for unemployment that same day. During the pandemic, and while receiving unemployment checks, Tony and I were able to save up a lot of cash. We were thinking about buying a house. I thought it was a brilliant idea to invest. I was in charge of picking the location. I don't know why he did that, because I was thinking out-of-state. I said, "How about we move to Atlanta, Georgia."

Tony's eyes opened wide and he replied, "Let's go." A few days later, while COVID is spreading fast, we are on the road to Georgia. We stopped in Memphis, Tennessee, for food, gas and to rest, but an hour later we were back on the road. The craziest thing about his whole ride was that we didn't have housing yet. We stayed in a hotel while we looked for houses to buy. With the market being so expensive, and the pandemic going on, it was hard to find a house because it was all about virtual meetings. No one wanted to be available, face-to-face during that time. Tony and I continued to search, until we finally got our break.

We found housing with an option to rent or buy, we quickly jumped on it after we viewed the place, which was perfect for us: with three bedrooms, two baths. The garage was connected to the house, which was a plus, so we decided to get it. The same day we received the keys to our house. Soon after we went back to our hotel room, where we spent our last night. The next morning, we gathered our belongings and checked out, going forward towards our new home.

Everything in the house was brand new or remodeled. I didn't have to do much but put my love into it. Now that the work was done, we had to go back to Minnesota because we still had our apartment there. We didn't want to drive back so we left our car in the driveway of our new house, and we flew back to Minnesota to get the rest of our things. Once there, we started to clean and pack. Our cars and big furniture remained in Minnesota. We decided not to move it all by ourselves so we hired movers who were able to move our cars and furniture across the country. I was so excited to move back to Georgia. Here are three reasons why I moved back to Georgia:

1. To finish what I started years ago in the music business,
2. Being at peace because we were away from all the drama in Minnesota, and
3. To start fresh with Tony Cordell.

Moving back to Georgia was the best decision that I could have made. I was able to heal in peace. I let my kids know what we decided to do before I left, but they didn't realize how serious I was about the move until I was gone. When things started to sink in, they weren't happy, but I had to live my life.

For three years before we moved to Georgia, Tony had to deal with my family's mess. Three years was a long time to be in madness, so I decided to get rid of it all.

I decided to choose me and my happiness for once.

As it is written, "Where there is good, evil is present." I'm a firm believer in that saying because my 25-year-old son went to jail for burglary. He served a year in prison, away from his wife and kids. It was a selfish act on his behalf.

Once out, he started going back into the streets with his gang members. I thought he was changing—because he has a wife and kids. Since when my son was just 12-years-old, he started getting into trouble. He was always in and out of jail, but now that he was 25, he should know right from wrong—or least think about his family. I say it again: That was a selfish act on his behalf.

My son was now in jail at the time of my move, and I'd barely heard from him. He's been in jail for about two years now—but when he was about to get released, the prosecutors didn't let him leave because of a murder charge that he had pleaded guilty to. The man he killed didn't deserve it. It was so crazy that the man died March 1, 2022—the same day my mom died in 1992. It couldn't get any crazier than this, and I was really, really upset. I couldn't believe my son took someone's life. That deeply broke my heart, and I've became sick for a couple days because it was just devastating—and to know how the other people felt was an understatement…I felt their pain. Now my only son is in prison serving his sentence, expecting to get out in the year 2039—which is sad because his children will be grown adults then. But my son has to learn what he did wasn't okay—and I pray that he comes to his senses—and that God forgives him.

His imprisonment made me question if I failed him as his mother—but then I realized he failed me as my son.

My son missed out, as usual, because he couldn't seem to get it together. I hated this happening to my grandkids and his wife because they didn't deserve it. However, I provided what my son couldn't, and while my son was in prison, the girls and I spent the holidays together.

However, I barely heard from my son in prison, and my daughters were still out of control—and would call me about the dumbest things. They would even call complaining about their dad. They would always try and put me in the middle of confusion. When I wouldn't participate in the drama, they would disrespect me. It had become so bad, sometimes to a point where I was in tears. They tried to make me feel guilty for getting a divorce., blaming me for the actions of my ex-husband. He felt like if he wasn't with me, then he's not doing it for the kids. I know that's what he thought because my adult children were calling me for money all the time.

Meanwhile one of my daughters came to visit me in Georgia. I was shocked because she's the one who was never happy for me. I know she came just to see how I was living. I assumed it was awesome for her because she was able to fly state-to-state. Her presence puzzled and confused me, but I stayed positive and happy because I was glad she came. I wanted all my children to see something different in life, and that's what I did. She stayed for a couple of days before going home.

Soon after, Tony found a job here in Georgia, and I found a job two months after. Tony was working in a warehouse, and I was working at a waffle restaurant. I never thought in a million years I'd be working there. It was crazy how I landed the job. I was going there every day for a cheesesteak sandwich. I was there so much the cooks knew what I wanted before I asked. During the process, the manager of the restaurant asked me if I wanted a job, and my response was, "Why not!" I was getting bored anyway, needing something to do. I was excited because I was now officially a Georgia resident. My first day at work was challenging because I was around new people. I've never had a problem with meeting new friends because I am a people person. I was able to quickly befriend one person who was sweet to me.

However, the other workers saw me as a threat, I understood why: because I was different. I came to work clean and fresh every day, because where I come from, first impression is important, especially in an interview. There was one episode where one of the workers wanted to fight me. I was brand new to Georgia so I didn't want to fight. I wasn't about to go to jail in Georgia, so I walked away. The managers saw what had happened, but they never took action. After that I knew I was headed for battle. The restaurant was full of drama queens and lost souls. I didn't quit though, because I was bringing home money every day from tips. It had taken me two weeks to learn the restaurant's "language"—and after that, it was full speed ahead.

I started to meet new people, and as a waitress, I was always in somebody's face. The customers loved me, and said I had good customer service—and that I have a smile that's out of this world. This caused my tips to go up, and I appreciated it. I was getting blessed with big tips, and this made the other workers upset because I was new and making more tips than them. They started talking behind my back, causing confusion on the job. It didn't bother me because I had only eight hours with them. I didn't have to sleep or eat with them after work, so I kept it moving.

A week later a customer walked in the restaurant as I was selecting music to play on the jukebox—and had played a song he liked. He started a conversation by asking me how old I was. I told him my age, and he said "No way, you look so young." I chuckled a little and said yeah, but I'm all woman. Soon after, I became the restaurant's DJ. The customers would come in and hand me money to select the music—just to rock the house on the jukebox. I was happy, too, because I was tired of spending my own money in the jukebox. However; I loved music, so I really didn't mind the cost—as long as the customers were satisfied.

The next day while at work, the same customer walked in. Johnny orders the same breakfast all the time, so before he could sit down, I had already called in his order. He always ordered a certain breakfast the restaurant was known for it. I brought the food to his table, and he stopped me in action. Johnny asked me to sit down for a second and talk with him. I had a few minutes because I didn't have any more customers at the time. He started to tell me what he was into, and told me that he writes movie scripts. To my surprise he was onto something, and with my skills and his vision, we could do business. He had a project in mind, and wondered, "Did I know of an R&B singer?" I said that yes, my daughter has strong vocals. He then asked me if there was any way he could hear her.

When I pulled up one of her YouTube videos, Johnny was amazed. He instantly wanted me to contact her to set up a meeting. I told him that she lives in Minnesota, and she has three kids. I added that her life isn't set up like that, and she would need some time. He understood, so we went on to talk about his project. At the end of our conversation, we shook hands—and things moved forward from there. As soon as I returned home, I called my daughter and asked how she would like to come to Atlanta. When I told the reason why, she excitedly answered, "Yes, I would like too, but I have to get her children situated first." I replied, "Of course you do." Before we hung up the phone, I told her to stay in contact. I had in mind to book her a flight to Atlanta, because this was business. Later that day, my daughter called me with the good news that the children's father would keep them. I said, "Cool, I'll see you tomorrow."

I booked her flight, and I called Johnny who is now my new business partner, informing him of her arrival, and he was excited. The next day I picked my daughter up from the airport. I saw the excitement in her, because she knew *it was going to be good for her future*. We went to my house so she could freshen up, because later we had a meeting. When we arrived at the meeting, everyone introduced themselves. My daughter sang for him, and he was impressed. We chilled for a while afterwards to have food and drinks. I had to be at work at 7:00 a.m., so we all departed. The next day, I woke up at 5:00 a.m. to get dressed for work. Everyone in the house was still asleep. I had a routine every morning: make coffee, watch the news for a while, and 45 minutes before my shift, I would shower and do my hair.

It's 6:55 a.m. as I'm getting ready to walk out of the door. I kissed Tony goodbye. I go to the guest room to tell my daughter I love her, and I'll see her later. My job was three minutes away, and it seems like I'm always late. The manager didn't mind too much, because he knew that I was a good worker, doing my job and doing it well, and it showed. During my shift, I get a call from Johnny, who had set up a meeting with a producer, singer, and songwriter. He wanted my daughter to attend, he told me what time, and it was set.

It started to get busy, and I didn't have time to call my daughter. Time had gone by so fast that already it was the end of my shift. I went home and told my daughter the news that we had a meeting at 6:00 p.m. I was exhausted from work so I relaxed a little, and had two-and-a-half hours to do so. My daughter was wide awake, too excited to relax. I gave her my car keys, and she went sightseeing. I gave her a time to come back, because in Atlanta, "everything" is far away.

Soon after, Tony, my daughter and I were on our way to the meeting. When we arrived, my business partner was outside in the parking lot. We all walked in together to the VIP section, "which was nice." As we sat down, I recognized one of the singers. He was a part of one of my favorite R&B groups. My daughter had no idea who he was because he was way before her time. I explained to her who he was, but still she gave me a look of no recognition. Anyway, the meeting continued, we talked about a lot of different things. My daughter had the honor to sing in front of Freddy, the promoter/Artist Recruiter (AR). He liked what he had heard. I know about the music business, so I asked questions—like a manager—and a mother who's protecting her cub. As we were wrapping up the meeting, we hadn't come up with an agreement so no contracts were signed. I wasn't about to waste my or my daughter's time. I believe if it doesn't make dollars, it doesn't make sense, so we left and headed for home.

The next morning Terry, a vocal trainer, called. He asked if he could train and work with my daughter. He had been in the meeting the night before, so he heard her vocals. He knew she had a gift. We talked for a brief second, and we set up a meeting for later that day. I walked to the room where my daughter was sleeping. I told her about the meeting we have, and she was excited. Hours went by, and soon we were off to the meeting. When we arrived at our destination in east Atlanta, the outside of the building was nice, the inside was a top-notch recording studio. Only celebrities were allowed inside, and everything was by appointment only. We looked around as the promoter was giving us a tour. We liked what we saw, so we continued to tour. The meeting was finally at hand, we talked and laughed for a minute to get more acquainted with each other. We had a few drinks, and now it was time for business. The meeting was going well—until Terry asked to be paid for his services.

I was shocked, and my eyes were big and ready to pop out my sockets. I calmed down and was in deep thought. I thought to myself that this man asked for my daughter, so why are we paying for this? We debated for a while, but I wasn't happy at all. Although things then became kind of shaky, my daughter and I came to an agreement that she would pay for her future. We called the promoter, set up a meeting, and we met at the restaurant where I worked.

We walked inside the restaurant, ordered lunch, and began to talk. Terry reached for his briefcase to pull out the contract. I read over it, it looked and sounded like a plan for my daughter. The contract stated that my daughter would be working with mainstream R&B singers. The contract also stated she would have a songwriter, many hours of vocal training—and a hit single. I was more excited than my daughter because I felt like *this was it*. We signed the contract and left happy. The very next day, my daughter was called to start her session. We arrived at the studio and began to work. I, on the other hand, was meeting with Freddy, the promoter/AR. We talked for a minute before I gave him $2,000 for my daughter's career. He had asked for $7,000, which wasn't bad for all the things he had in mind for her. I thought it was a good thing due to the fact that the promoter "knew people." I saw with my own eyes that he knew big names in the industry. As a matter of fact, he was in a couple of major plays, streaming all across America.

I trusted his word, and I continued to pay money—*but then sadly I found out that he was only out for himself.* By this time, I had given Freddy $5,000 total. He wasn't on top of what he said he was going to do for my daughter. He only wanted money! He started ignoring my phone calls. I later found out that he was in California, doing other things besides what his contract stated. Time was running out, and my daughter had to get home to her children. The promoter wasn't communicating with us so she had to leave.

Unfortunately, my daughter went home with lost hopes. I felt deeply ashamed, like it was my fault for trusting someone who was up to no good in the first place. I should have known better. I tried calling, seeking a refund, but never received an answer. I prayed about it—but it was a lesson learned. It was a red flag from the start, and I should've paid more attention.

As time went by, I still worked at the waffle restaurant. Usually I work on to-go orders, but this one particular day I was an in-house server. When the next customer walked in, I asked if he was ready to order. He replied yes, and placed his order. He asked me, "What are you doing here?" I replied with a chuckle of surprise. "Ummm, I work here" (haha). He then asks, "What else do you do?" I broke down and told him, so he asked me if I wanted to come work for him. I considered only because he was someone in high demand as an agent. We exchanged phone numbers.

The next day after work I received a text message from him. He invited Tony and me to his work place. We agreed, and he sent the address. When we arrived, my eyes lit up with excitement. His workplace was about two blocks long. It's like we walked into Tyler Perry Studios, it was huge and gave off a Hollywood feeling. He took us on a tour, and wow, the things I was witnessing. It is an entertainer's dream, everything in one place. I had told myself that I wasn't getting back into the music business, but after seeing the studio that expands two blocks long—I was all in. When I was introduced to the team, they greeted me with love. I was going to places I never even knew about in Atlanta, getting treated like I was a very important person (VIP) at its best. During the process of being introduced to some heavy hitters in the music industry, Tony and I were getting out-of-town visitors. I thought it was the perfect timing, because I knew where to go in Atlanta for excitement. I certainly knew where all the good eating spots were. One of my favorite restaurants in Lithonia, Georgia, is called, "This Is It"—one of the best soul food joints in Georgia. I was a faithful customer, going at least three times a week.

By now, Tony and I have been living in Georgia for three years. I became a veteran working at the waffle restaurant, and every customer knew who I was. I loved my customers, and they loved me back. About an hour later, I went outside for a break. I looked for my lighter so I can have a smoke, and when I looked up, this woman appeared out of nowhere, with tears running down her face. My love instincts kicked in, and instantly I grabbed to hug her. After I gave her a shoulder to cry on, I asked her what was wrong. She replied to me with a sad look, "I just moved up here from another state, I'm running from an abusive relationship." She also stated that she needed help, she has no money for food. She also went on to say that she is renting a room and needs money for rent. I dropped everything that I was doing to cater to her needs at the moment. I told her we are hiring, and I asked if she was interested. She replied yes, and I took her inside. I told her to have a seat while I go get the manager. She waited patiently, and the manager interviewed her. As I can see and hear, the interview is going great. I knew she was about to be hired by the way they shook hands at the end. She was excited, and I was excited for her as well. Before she left, she walked over to me and gave me the biggest hug. She said, "Thank you, you have a heart of gold." She went home happy.

The next day I see the woman at work. With joy in her eyes, I knew she was glad to already be working in less than 24 hours. Then the manager informed me I was to train her. I was happy to train her, so we started immediately. For a few hours she was shadowing behind me, just to get the feel of working at there. It was time for my break and she followed me outside. We got to know each other, and we became best friends, more like sisters. We started spending more time together outside of work. She came over to my house—and the conversations were getting way personal. She explained to me about her life, and what she wanted to do in life. I'm glad she shared it with me, because we share some of the same life experiences. She also told me she was an actor, which blew my mind because I had connections. Days before I was invited to this event, and I thought that she would be a good candidate for the event. When I invited her to join me, she was excited.

A couple days later we met at my house, and we went off to the Black Wall Street Event Center. We walked inside of the event, and I introduced her to a couple of people. One person there stood out to me—she was the host of the event. She's been hosting for many years, and has been busy in the entertainment business for a long time. Soon after the event was over, we started to network. I walked up to the person who hosted the event, introduced my friend, and now she has been busy in the business in every way. Let's just say she's the "Queen of Atlanta." Look at us, God! Ha, ha, now we've become best friends.

My vision for Georgia became realistic, and people would walk up to me out of nowhere—wanting me to show them the ropes about the entertainment world. They knew I had a little something under my belt by the way I carried myself, and from hearing people talk about me. They would say that girl who works at the waffle place has connections and involvement with some big names. I really didn't...but I just knew people who knew people—so I guess it was enough for them to get started. It's crazy how I don't care about being in the world of entertainment anymore; however, I like to see other people live out their dreams.

CHAPTER 20
MAKING CONNECTIONS AT THE WAFFLE RESTAURANT

Working at the waffle place has opened many doors for me—sometimes doors I didn't want to open. I had the honor of doing what I love, and that's to serve people. I didn't want to pursue the music business anymore. I had different plans, but one of my co-workers had the desire to become a rap artist. You can pretty much see the hunger in a person, and how badly they want to be successful. My co-worker was one of them. I figured since I had the connection, I'll share it with my co-worker.

The next day he didn't come into work, but his sister did. His sister was the chef and a good cook. I walked up to her and asked about her brother, saying I wanted to set up a meeting with him. Excited, she agreed to inform her brother what's all about to take place. Our eight-hour shift was over, and we said our goodbyes for the day. The next day I went to work. Neither one was there, but I didn't think anything of it. I was on the schedule, so I started my shift. A few hours into work, the morning rush is over and both my co-workers walked through the front door together.

Since business was slow, I took my break early. We greeted one another with hugs, and the meeting began. I asked him how serious he was—and was he ready for what's next? I explained to them what the ups and downs are in this line of business. They both understood, and were prepared for take-off. Soon after, I contacted my industry connection to set up a meeting for my coworker and me. The meeting was set, we met and sat around a big white table that was meant for the bosses. My coworker's eyes lit up with joy, because he had never been in this type of setting—especially now that he had to talk about himself. The meeting continued for a while, and everything sounded great. My co-worker was one step closer to his dream.

Before the meeting was over, I had one more thing to show him. When I took him on a tour of the building, he was in awe mode. It had everything he desired, including a recording studio and everything else to go with the business of any kind. After all that was over, it was time to part ways. He was one happy camper, *and I loved seeing it*. A few days later my co-worker contacted me to ask if I could manage him. I replied, and with all due respect, said, "It's not something that I'm into anymore." He respectfully understood, but I gave him a suggestion—that his sister should be his manager, as it'll save money and stress. He took my advice, and his sister is now his manager. We had a few more meetings, and then they were off on their own. His sister stepped up, and now he has music that's circulating on all social media—from music videos and collaborations, and they are doing pretty well.

Sometimes in life, all we need is for someone to show us how, and encourage us to be great.

With a humble heart, I'm proud to be a part of their success. *One thing for certain, and two things for sure, in life be careful how you treat people. You never know who you're dealing with.* While working at the waffle place I've seen and gone through it all—the good, the bad and the ugly, and still I survived.

It is now two months into the year 2024. January and February have gone by, and we're in the month of March. I've decided to have a big birthday party for myself, even though it is three months away. I like to plan early, just to give myself time mentally and financially. My party included hiring a live disc jockey and a host for my event, plus free food and drinks. The theme was out of this world. I love wigs so I had a wigs-on-wigs birthday party bash. All the ladies had to wear a wig of their choice. It was very unique, I paid for an online flier and the party was set.

Meanwhile, Tony and I get an unexpected visitor from our hometown who was attending a business meeting here in Georgia. After the visitor had finished the meeting, we were asked to pick him up. Our visitor had one day left in Georgia so it was decided that he'll spend it with us. We went out to dinner, and had a discussion about moving back to our hometown. I was really confused because I was just getting started. I made friends, had plans and had my own things going on. The conversation had gone deep, deep to a point where it was an offer that we couldn't refuse. When dinner was over, we went back to our house. It was late so we all went to bed. I laid back in the bed, with Tony next to me.

I asked him with a wandering mind: "Tony, how do you feel about moving back home?" He replied, "I don't know yet." I rolled over to face the wall and thought to myself…hmmmm, I'll sleep on it, and see how I feel the next morning. Now it's morning, and our visitor has an afternoon flight to catch. I had to work early, so they were still asleep. I was thinking about the conversation we had at dinner the day before. I was still indecisive about what I wanted to do. As I started my work shift, I kind of forgot about the conversation. Then we became so busy I didn't notice Tony and our visitor were in the restaurant. He came to tell me he's on his way to the airport to drop off our visitor. He kissed me and left. At the end of my shift, I head home where I find Tony sitting on the sofa watching television. I slipped off my shoes to get comfortable, and I began to ask him about the conversation we had a day before. After a long discussion, we came up with something. Yes, we decided to move back home, and I was kind of disappointed, but that changed quickly. All I could think about are my grandchildren and kids. Being closer to them was my main goal for going back, besides I already had nine grandchildren at the time. Tony and I decided on a date to move back home. By this time, we've been a resident of Georgia for three years and 11 months. We had decided to move after my birthday party on June 15th—marking our four years as Georgia residents. We would have left sooner but I had a party to throw, and I've already spent too much money to cancel it, so I was stuck there for a few more months.

During the process of trying to move, and also having a birthday party, was overwhelming.

We had a three-bedroom house, with every room furnished from front to back. I started selling and giving stuff away. I never knew how much stuff I had until it was time to pack up. It took us two months to clear out our house, and I was exhausted just looking at it. Going to work, moving, and also promoting my party was a lot—enough to make a person think she is going to lose her mind. After we sold all our furniture, I took three days off from work. Tony and I had decided to bring some of our belongings back to our hometown. We wanted to move as few things as possible before our permanent move. We arrived in our hometown after driving for 16 hours, and dropped our stuff off at our new home—located on a lake, and came with a boat. I was too excited, because I grew up fishing on that lake. The thought of knowing where I was headed was jaw-dropping, making me more excited to move.

Back in Georgia it was "crunch time," with just two weeks to get ready for the party; then the move. My mind is all over the place, with my real-life issues—and with all the madness and drama going on at work, I knew my time was up in Georgia. The devil got really busy, attack after attack, to a point that my job was on the line. I had only a few days left working there, so I kept my cool because one thing about me—I'm going to exit on good soil. I'll leave on good terms because when I'm spoken of, it's nothing but goodness.

June 10, 2024 was my last day working at the waffle place. I said my goodbyes, and it was a wrap. For four days I finished packing for our permanent move back home. With my birthday party being in 24 hours, I had a lot on my plate. Some of my family members flew into town to celebrate with me. I was busy, busy, busy. They came over for a while, we visited, ate dinner; then they were off to their hotels.

My special day has arrived, and I'm excited. I have both a real cute wig and outfit ready for the night. I hoped everything was set, as our things were packed, and we were ready to hit the road the next day.

My party started at eight and ended at one a.m. The people there were my friends and some family, and we had a ball. I had a live DJ, live performances, and someone hosting my event. At the end of the day, it turned out wonderful, and I'm glad I did it.

The party is over and the night has ended. I'm saying goodbye to my friends who were very surprised because they didn't know I was leaving in the morning—actually, in a few hours. I hugged them, and asked them to stay in contact.

Tony and I went to our hotel room because we had moved out of our house. We slept some; then soon we were on the road back to our hometown in Minnesota. It took us a few weeks to get settled at our new house on a lake—time I gladly spent with my grandkids and kids. We went fishing, boating, swimming, and four-wheeling. We had fun for the summer; and it felt good to walk out our back door and face a lake.

CHAPTER 21
WE'RE BACK IN MINNESOTA

Summer is soon over, and then school will be in session. It is now August 2024, and I have become bored so I decided to sign up for school. Although I've already graduated, I felt like I needed to refresh my memory. Once enrolled, I did some testing to find out if I had forgotten what I've learned. I've been out of school for 15 years or so, so I'm proud of myself. The following week I was a student, and I had the honor of meeting my teachers. I had two classes: writing and reading. My writing teacher asked me. "What are you doing here?" I replied, "To get my mind refreshed for a job—and also gain digital literacy."

When my "good" test scores really disqualified me from being an actual student there, my teacher suggested I do something else. We talked one-on-one, allowing him to get to know me better.

I told him my story, and he suggested that I write a book. I thought about it, long and hard, because at age 47, I didn't know a thing about typing. Then my dear teacher suggested I take typing lessons. The next morning at school, he gave me a computer so I could start my typing lessons. Even though I was so determined to be able to type, it had taken me three weeks to just get the hang of using the computer. Unbelievable, soon I was typing, and it was all self-taught. My teacher came to me and cheerfully said, "You did it! Now it's time to start writing your book, Tamica."

God in My Life...

Now filled with confidence, I started. Writing this book was challenging for me—as I looked back, *I realized that I've been through a lot in life.* The battles I've faced, from the age of 10 to being 40, weren't pleasant. Let's just say that as I grew in knowledge, I understood that I had been "on trial" for 30 years. *I fought the good fight,* as Peter in the Bible said to himself.

I grew to know that God has been with me forever—and I didn't care who was against me. Talking about having tough skin is an understatement, as God himself created me to become strong. God's battles are not for the weak, and I'm a soldier in his army. I'm so thankful God gave me wisdom at such a young age. The bricks that were meant to destroy me, God was using to build my future. As I understood the assignment, the test wasn't easy. It had taken me 30 years on trial, and now I'm living in my tribulation—the cause of my troubles and suffering. I'm engaged to Tony Cordell, with a wedding date set for fall, 2026. Only this time it's real mature love! Love conquers our future…

What we go through in life can either make us or break us. I had the honor of spending 14 years of my life with my mother. When I was young, she was a strong-willed person, which rubbed off on me. Sadly, after she and my dad divorced, she was so very sad and lonesome,

and she let down her guard from being the strong woman we grew up with.

That's how the evil Preston entered her life. He first brought her joy for a couple weeks, and then everything went downhill until the day he killed her. Every day I ask, "Why did she stay with such a horrible person?" Since that awful day, I have worked hard as an adult to love myself first and foremost, and take care of myself, being diligent to find and choose a man who would never hurt me or my children.

With the power of God and his divine mercy, I was chosen. God chose me to do exactly what I'm assigned to do today. My life is not in vain, and neither is my story. I'm hoping I can inspire my readers to believe in yourselves—*knowing God is real and always in control.* The things we face in life are only temporary, the good or the bad. I'm a firm believer that God sacrifices the things closest to you to get the attention of his people. I believe I was stripped from one love to have love for others, even when I felt like earlier in life, no one loved me back. God saved me…my prayers are forever answered.

I persevered, I'm now an author, hoping to become a motivational speaker someday.

As I close this story, I appreciate the love and support I receive from my family. Without you guys, I wouldn't have a story. GOD IS EVERYTHING!!!!

Going Forward…

I'll never forget my sadness, grief and sense of loss…
but I am still moving ahead. – Tamica

WHAT I HAVE LEARNED IN THOSE 30 YEARS

Final Thoughts and Advice to Read, Remember, and Act Upon if Relevant:

- To the women in an abusive relationship, *you are not alone.* Lift up your voice and ask for help, as it is available. Speak with someone today!

- If you know of someone being abused, reach out to her. A lot of resources are available online or by phone—or in person in the area where you live. HELP IS NEAR YOU.

- Read all the extra information on domestic violence below and throughout the book, so you are prepared, aware, and know your rights and how to proceed if needed.

- You never need to apologize for showing your grief.

- You can have a better future by remembering your past.

- Always make sure *you love yourself first and foremost* so the scale doesn't tip—and someone else has control over you and your life.

- If you have a gut feeling about something, don't ignore the signs. Always pay full attention to that

person's body language, energy, facial expressions,
and how you're treated in different situations.

- When I weigh my personal sadness of having my mother murdered by her husband (not our father)—a woman who also had to watch him physically abuse her two children—I am glad that now I feel strong enough to be a community spokesperson against domestic violence.

- Memories of Mom pop into my head every once in a while. I am glad some of them are more of our life "before Preston" entered it, with such horrifying results. Appreciate your mom when you have her, help her if she needs it, and learn from her mistakes.

- Our son who is in prison for a long time, made many bad decisions, not uncommon for young people today—especially those whose father demonstrates only negative lifestyles—and those without positive role modeling provided by mothers.

- If your husband isn't providing good examples for your children—only bad and dangerous ones—determine that you'll provide enough for both parents.

- If your husband is in fact providing very negative and dangerous paths for your kids to follow, you have to be twice as strong and very alert to how your children are living.

- Girls/women who have watched their mothers be abused need to understand what to look for in a new relationship, and what to avoid when selecting a boyfriend; then a husband.

- Appreciate the members of your extended family who willingly help you with your children when you need it.

- If a young man who is a husband and father is killed, try to find some ways you can help her. Consider holidays, etc. when the man is missed the most.

- If a relative or friend has her partner/other parent in jail, prison, or some other kind of "lock-up situation," find ways you can support her and offer needed help.

ACKNOWLEDGMENTS

To my dad—you are the best. You never gave up on me. Thanks for still being in my life.

To my three daughters, you have become wonderful adults—responsible, supportive, and caregiving.

To my teacher, Mr. Green, thank you so much for believing in me, motivating and pushing me to write. I'll never forget that you gave my story a A++.

To my fiancé, Tony Cordell, thanks for encouraging me to finalize the book, and reminding me I am accomplishing "my dream."

To my niece, Cara Sutton, who used her talent to design the three silhouettes for the cover.

To my editor, Connie Anderson (www.WordsandDeedsInc.com) who spent extra time helping make the book be the "best possible." She ensured that my messages were strong as they reached out to the reader.

When I told my dad, who lives in Arizona, that I had written a book about my life and that of the family, he said, "I am so proud of you." Then I thought, "Heck, I'm proud of me, too! Learning to type, then typing the words for an entire book—and it's not just the words but making sure what's important is included."

DID YOU KNOW?

Information shared from *MariasVoice.org*—a non-profit formed by parents whose daughter was murdered by her husband

- One in four women in the U.S. will be targeted by an abusive partner in their lifetime.
- Female victims most commonly experience violence first between the ages of 18-24 (38.8%); followed by age 11-17 (22.4%); then 35-44 (66.8%) and ages 45 plus, (2.5%).
- Women account for two out of three murder victims killed by an intimate partner.
- One out of five (16%) murder victims were killed by an intimate partner.
- One in five teenage girls said they have been in a relationship where their boyfriend threatened violence or self-harm if she wanted to break up with him.
- It's estimated that every year 3.3 million children in the U.S. witness violence against a female in their family—mother or female caretaker.

In my home state of Minnesota, 35 percent of law enforcement calls are domestic disputes.

RESOURCES

1. National Domestic Violence Hotline. Languages: English, Spanish and 200-plus more through interpretation services. Phone: 1-800-799-7233

2. Violence Free Minnesota's Get Help. Day One Crisis Hotline. Phone: 1-866-223-1111

3. Battered Women Justice Project (BWJP) Online help
   If you, or someone you know needs to know more about domestic abuse, read this excellent website: https://www.healthline.com/health/post-separation-abuse – article is called "11 Common Post-Separation Abuse Tactics."

   The First Signs of Domestic Violence

   Refer to the Duluth Wheel: Website has excellent list of things you should know:

   https://www.theduluthmodel.org/wheels/

   This non-profit developed this wheel to give more clarity. They divide violence—both physical and sexual—into these eight categories of having Power and Control by using:
   1. Intimidation
   2. Emotional abuse
   3. Isolation

4. Minimizing, denying and blaming
5. Children
6. "Male privilege"
7. Economic abuse
8. Coercion and threats

This website gives more answers:
https://www.healthline.com/health/post-separation-abuse

PHASE 1: Tension is building: The abuser is argumentative, angry, uses verbal criticism, swearing and angry gestures. Sometimes the abuser will use coercion and threats, or minor fights might occur.

- POWER AND CONTROL: Guilt, blaming, minimizing and denial. He hits, slaps, pushes, kicks, holds you down, pulls your hair, or physically hurts you. And often he threatens you with weapon or even threatens self-harm.
- ISOLATION: Controlling contact with family and friends. He checks your phone, controls who you see and where you go.
- EMOTIONAL ABUSE: Intimidation and threatening looks, also actions like destroying property, coercion and threats.
- VERBAL: Writing threats to hurt or hill. Using kids or loved ones to "guilt you." He also puts you down, says you are crazy, calls you names, and humiliates you.

- KEY STATISTICS: Prevalence, 41 percent of women—and 26 percent of men—experience intimate violence.
- LIFE IMPACTS: Over 61 million women have experienced physical violence from an intimate partner.
- REPORTING: A significant number of domestic violence incidents go unreported—with only a small percent of victims seeking help. Law enforcement and other services are available.
- AGE: Women from ages 18-24 generally experience the highest rates of violence—including physical and sexual violence, as well as stalking and psychological aggression.
- RISK FACTORS: Women with disabilities and women in certain age groups are at higher risk of experiencing domestic violence.
- ECONOMIC IMPACT: Violence experienced in the U.S. population is estimated to be 3.6 trillion women and children. One woman or girl is killed every 10 minutes by their intimate partner.

Together We Can Change Lives

ABOUT THE AUTHOR

Tamica Barnett

Tamica has a great sense of humor and loves camping, fishing, being in nature, and animals—especially llamas. She also enjoys cooking.

She graduated from Broadway Adult Basic Education Center in Minneapolis and later attended Globe University/Minnesota School of Business as an adult student.

Professionally, Tamica is an event planner, music artist manager, self-made hip-hop promoter, and the owner of her own record label.

Her message is one she believes everyone needs to hear: *Never take life for granted, never let a person dim the light that God gave you —and stand firm in your belief.*

If you meet Tamica, you quickly see her determination. Whatever she sets her mind to, she pursues wholeheartedly. At age 46 she taught herself to type, and with encouragement from her teachers, she began writing her life story—hoping one day it may become a movie.

Tamica and Tony Cordell are engaged to be married. She has four adult children, one son and three daughters—and eleven grandchildren, along with a step-grandson in college.

Because of her family's personal experiences, Tamica hopes to become an advocate for those affected by domestic violence, especially women of all backgrounds.

Silence helps the abuser, not the victim.